eurolingua
Deutsch

THE LEARNER'S HANDBOOK

D1696535

Cornelsen

eurolingua **Deutsch** THE LEARNER'S HANDBOOK

Part A: Lutz Rohrmann and Susanne Self
Part B and C: Lutz Rohrmann

Translated by: Mark Eriksson; assisted by: Christine House

Pedagogic consultants:
Dr. Hansjörg Frommer (VHS Karlsruhe), Dr. Hermann Funk (GhK Kassel),
Michael Koenig (GhK Kassel), Sabine Rosenfeld (KVHS Saarlouis),
Jacqueline Sword (Leine-VHS, Hemmingen), Dr. Erich Zehnder (Mainz)

Lay-out and cover: Regelindis Westphal
Illustrations: Laurent Lalo

Cover photo: Berlin, Bahnhof Zoo

1st Edition 1998 ✔   Impression 4th 3rd 2nd 1st   Year 01 2000 99 98

© this edition: 1998 Cornelsen Verlag, Berlin
© original edition: 1996 Migros Genossenschafts-Bund,
Koordinationsstelle der Klubschulen, Zürich
Authors of the original edition: Hermann Funk and Michael Koenig
Consultants of original edition:
Daniel Coste, Anthony Fitzpatrick, Henri Holec, Ernesto Martín Peris,
René Richterich, Jan Van Ek

All rights reserved. No part of this book may be used or reproduced
in any manner whatsoever without written permission.

Composition: Satzinform, Berlin
Repro studio: Satzinform, Berlin
Print: Druck-Centrum Fürst, Berlin
Binder: Fritzsche-Ludwig, Berlin

ISBN 3-464-20999-7
Order number 209997

gedruckt auf säurefreiem Papier, umweltschonend hergestellt aus chlorfrei gebleichten Faserstoffen

INTRODUCTION

This book is designed to help you learn German. It is meant for your use when you are working alone at home and as an aid in finding your own way of learning. In addition, you can use it as a reference when you run into problems with grammar or when you want to prepare yourself for particular situations where you have to speak German. The Learner's Handbook is a good companion for all three volumes of **euro**lingua **Deutsch**. There are three main parts:

Learning to Learn It is best to read Part A of the Learner's Handbook once at the beginning of the course. It gives you important tips on how you can learn more effectively and will help you to establish a style of learning that works best for you. Here we have put together a number of tips and techniques for learning that will be used again and again during the course.

Language in Use In Part B you will find a large variety of expressions and dialogues, organized systematically, that are helpful in those important everyday situations. For example, here you can look up how to greet people, how to begin a business letter or one to a friend, or what to say at the doctor's.

Grammar This part deals with grammar and pronunciation. In Part C we have put together an overview of the language structures that are presented in all three volumes. Whenever you are not quite sure of the grammar rules, you can look them up here. The grammar presented is based on the requirements of the *Grundbaustein* and *Zertifikat Deutsch als Fremdsprache*.

Appendix Here you will find lists of numbers, measures and weights, verbs with prepositions, irregular verbs and the index.

How can you find what you are looking for?

Table of Contents *Page* 5

To find out how the information in the Learner's Handbook is organized, or to find more information about a specific topic, just look it up in the **table of contents**.

▶ Look at the table of contents and find out where the chapters on **Language in Use** and **Grammar** start and then thumb through them to see how they are organized.

Index *Page* 211

Here you can find important keywords from the Learner's Handbook. To find out more about a particular topic just look it up in the **index**.

Here are two examples:

1 Maybe you want to know how to greet someone in German. Just look in the index under greetings and find page number 52.

2 You have forgotten what the second person singular form of the verb sein is. Look up the verb sein or the key word irregular verbs in the index and you end up on page 209.

▶ Why not try it out right now? Look up the key word sich verabschieden (saying good-bye) and the question word wer (who).

Signs and symbols used in the Learner's Handbook

/ means that there are alternatives: Schöne Festage/Feiertage.

( ) indicates that the word(s) in brackets can be omitted: Das tut mir (sehr) Leid.

▲ draws attention to a particular problem.

▶ indicates that you should do something.

A, CH, D refer to language variants in Germany (D), Austria (A) and Switzerland (CH).

→ ⌑ this symbols lets you know you can find more information in another section of the Learner's Handbook. For example → ⌑ **C 47.2** means in section 47.2 of part C (**Grammar**) you will find more information.

TABLE OF CONTENTS

C GRAMMAR

Speaking and writing

Words and sentences

Word formation

Verbs

Nouns

Determiners and pronouns

APPENDIX

1   Learning to learn – why?

When you were at school you learnt a lot of different subjects, but one question seldom came up in class: How do people learn and how can I personally learn best? Today we know that learning can also be learnt and that when we consciously learn how to learn, we can save a lot of time and energy in the learning process (eg when learning a language). That is why we have emphasized this particular point in **eurolingua** and why there is a whole chapter in this book about **learning to learn.**

1.1   Learning on your own

You are learning German and of course you would like to be able to use what you have learnt outside the classroom. That is why it is important for you to know how you can continue to learn on your own, even when your teacher is not there to help you.

1.2   Finding your own way of learning

There are a lot of different ways of remembering things. Not everybody is successful using the same learning strategies. Once you have identified your own preferred learning style, you can learn much more quickly and effectively.
eurolingua cannot supply you with a "sure-fire" method, but we can help you to develop your own system or learning strategies.

2   Three key questions

2.1   Why am I learning German?

You have chosen a course for beginners that will give you a solid base in German. You almost certainly have particular likes and interests that made you want to learn German. Perhaps you need German for holidays in a German-speaking country or for your job. It could be that you are interested in German literature or that you have German friends. Every now and then during your **eurolingua** course you should think about your reasons for learning German – and compare them with those of the other participants in your class. This will help you to make the course work for you and to find those areas that correspond to your own interests and you can decide which aspects you want to work on more intensively on your own (eg everyday German, reading German literature, German at work, etc).

2.2 What learning style works best for me?

eurolingua can help you to learn German quickly and well. The way that is right for you depends on a lot of different factors:
- Do you already speak another foreign language?
- How have you learnt up to now? What learning experience do you already have?
- How important is it to you to learn German now? How intensively will you be able to deal with the course material?
- How much time do you have for – or are you willing to put into – learning German? Do you have time to do homework? Do you have a place where you can sit down and really concentrate?
- What kind of a learner are you? For example, do you like to try out new things right away or do you prefer to deal with the "theory" first? Do you remember things you hear or things you see better?

We present you with different tasks and activities and various tips and techniques for learning that can help you to learn. Just pick out what you can use and what makes the most sense to you.

2.3 What have I learnt so far and where do I go from here?

Every now and then during the course, sit down and think about how things are going. The following questions may help you to evaluate your progress. You could write them down in the front of the notebook you will be using for your German class or hang them over the desk where you study.

- Have I learnt what I wanted to?
- Have I been having fun learning?
- How much time have I spent learning German?
- What would I like to learn better?
- What is my next goal?
- How can I achieve it?

3 Four important components of the language class

3.1 Language in Use and Vocabulary

Step by step, you will learn how to make your-self understood in German in a variety of everyday situations (eg greeting people, reserving a hotel room, shopping ...).

Ich hätte gern drei Bananen.

3.2 Grammar

You will become acquainted with the rules that are important to help you learn German. Grammar is a tool which helps you to understand spoken and written texts – and to produce them yourself – more easily. As you learn to speak and write German better, you will find that you have to think about the rules less and less.

3.3 Cross-cultural learning: the German-speaking countries

When you learn a foreign language, you also learn about other cultures. During the course you will often make comparisons between the life and experiences of people in German-speaking countries and your own experi-ences. This also gives you a chance to see your own country and your own culture from another perspective and it promotes cross-cultural under-standing.

3.4 Learning to learn

Whilst you are learning German, you will find out how you, personally, best learn a foreign language. Many of the techniques for learning and studying, which you may well encoun-ter here for the first time, will be useful when you want to learn another language or continue your education in some other field.

4   Learning in class and at home

4.1   Working in groups and with a partner

In **euro**lingua you are often
asked to work with other
students in your class.
This presents you with
various advantages:
- Working in groups means
  you get more time to speak
  and practise. At the same time
  the teacher can use these periods
  to work individually with students who need special help.
- Most people express themselves more freely in a small group than in front of a lot of
  people.
- Independent learning is often more effective. When you work things out or look them
  up yourself, you remember them better.
- When you explain something to someone else in a small group, you also remember it
  better yourself.
- By exchanging your ideas in the group, you can also learn from the other students.
- And last but not least: in the modern business world, team work is becoming more and
  more important. By working in groups and with a partner in your German course, you
  improve your skills in team work.

4.2   Your teacher: a language and learning adviser

See your teacher as a learning adviser. For example ask for:
- additional explanations when you don't understand
  something;
- further exercises if you don't feel sure of something
  and would like to do additional work at home;
- more information when you are especially interested
  in a particular topic;

- tips on reading materials, dictionaries or newspapers and where you can get them;
- tips on how you can improve the way you learn and how you can overcome any learning
  difficulties;
- help if you have problems in your group.

Make sure you let your teacher know if you don't like something in class and make
suggestions for improvements.

4.3 German and your mother tongue in monolingual classes

The goal of a German class is to speak German as much as possible. As soon as you can, try to ask any questions you have in German – whether they are questions for other students or for the teacher. The more you say in German, the faster you learn to speak it. The course book presents many useful phrases and expressions for communicating in the classroom.
There are also times in class when you can and should use your mother tongue. Sometimes there are questions about German-speaking countries or inter-cultural issues that you are not able to discuss in German yet. It often makes sense, as well, to talk about grammar problems in your own language first and to compare German structures with those in your own language before practising them in German.

4.4 Learning on your own at home

Learning German at home is essential if you wish to learn the language well. Most tasks and exercises done in the classroom can also be done at home. It is even better if you can arrange to practise with someone else at home. The advantage of studying at home is that you can decide when you do it and the atmosphere at home may be more relaxed than in the classroom.
It is important to make sure that you have the proper atmosphere for learning.
– Think about when you can find that "quiet time" for studying German.
– Make sure that the people around you realize that the time you put aside for studying German is important to you and that they respect this.
– Find a place where you feel good and where it is quiet.
– Try to start each period that you study German with a relaxation activity. Close your eyes and (perhaps with some relaxing music) try to clear your mind of everything else, so that you will be able to concentrate on the task of learning German.

5 Picking up, processing and storing information

Put simply, learning means two things:
– Picking up information and incorporating it into things you already know.
– Taking care not to forget the things you have learnt.

For most of us, the second point is the main problem.

Whether or not you process the new information and keep it in your memory in the long run, depends on a lot of different factors (interest, motivation, what you already know, etc). In the following sections we would like to present two recommendations in more depth:

1 Use all of your senses to learn: (sight, hearing, touch, taste, smell).

2 Apply what you have learnt and review it regularly.

6 Using all of your senses to learn

The pictures symbolize different types of learners.

▶ Which type of learner do you see yourself as? Please tick the appropriate box.

All of us use our sensory channels (sight, hearing, taste, etc) in different ways. For one person sight is the most important, for the next it is hearing, and others can only remember something really well when they can touch it, too.
Of course everyone learns using all of their senses – only the emphasis is different. The better we use all of these channels, the easier it is for us to store new information. We suggest you actively exercise and develop learning techniques involving all of your senses to enable you to remember newly-learnt material more effectively.
We have compiled several learning techniques using the three most important senses.

6.1 Memorizing using your sense of sight

- Write down new words and try to remember how the words look.
- Label pictures.
- Draw pictures yourself and label them, at the same time saying the words out loud.
- Visualize: make mental connections between the words or expressions and vivid mental images.
- Hang up lists of new words around the house.
- Make groups of words that belong together thematically.
- Read as much as possible in German.

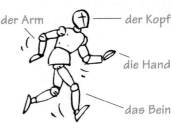

der Arm — *der Kopf*

die Hand

das Bein

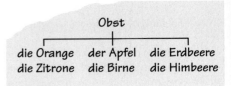

Obst

| *die Orange* | *der Apfel* | *die Erdbeere* |
| *die Zitrone* | *die Birne* | *die Himbeere* |

6.2 Memorizing using your sense of hearing

- Listen to the **euro**lingua **Deutsch** recordings over and over again.
- Repeat the words and sentences out loud.
- Record words on a cassette and listen to the recording several times.
- Listen to a dialogue more than once and take notes. Then, using your notes, try to reconstruct the dialogue out loud.
- Learn dialogues by heart and practise them out loud.
- Rehearse dialogues with the help of a cassette recorder. Speak the part of one speaker into the microphone, leaving space for the second speaker's answers. Then rewind the cassette and take on the role of the second speaker. At first read your part and then try it again from memory.
- Listen to as much German as possible: watch films in German (with or without sub-titles).
- Study together with one or two other students. Ask each other about words or practise dialogues together.
- Listen to German radio stations and songs. Even if you don't understand very much at the beginning, you will still be getting used to the sound of the language.

6.3 Memorizing using your senses of touch and motion

- Write a lot. For example, you can copy out texts leaving blanks that you can fill in later.
- Write out words and sentences that you want to learn.

- You will remember the names for things better if you touch them at the same time as you are learning their names.
- Learn the terms for actions (verbs) by doing the action at the same time as you repeat the word out loud.
- Write words in the air in order to remember them better.
- Turn your home into a picture dictionary. Stick labels with the appropriate words on your furniture and on other objects around the house.
- Memorize texts the way an actor learns a new role. Use your hands and feet. Speak softly and loudly, quickly and slowly and make the appropriate gestures and movements.
- Work with one or two others. Stage dialogues as roleplays, in which you act out the appropriate situations.

6.4 Processing new information

Memorizing new information is the first step in the learning process. This, however, is not enough to enable you to successfully use what you have learnt. You have to continually process the new words and structures, incorporating them into language you already know, thereby expanding your command of the language as a whole.

So don't be satisfied with just learning new material by heart. Try to actively process the new material and to use it in a variety of situations. In doing this, the following learning techniques may be of help to you:

- Look for grammatical regularities and check them by looking them up in the grammar section.
- Look for regularities in the way words are constructed. For example, the opposites of many adjectives are made using the prefix un– in German.
- Learn words by ordering them into groups according to principles that you think up yourself (word families, words connected to a particular theme, pairs of opposites, words with similar meanings, words with positive/negative associations, etc).

- Draw diagrams or networks of words from texts and use these to try to write a summary of the text later.
- Every now and then try to translate words and expressions into your mother tongue.
- Work with others and explain what you have learnt to each other.
- Make up your own exercises and exchange them with others in your class.
- Ask the most important question over and over again: Why?

7 Practising and revising

- Make a study plan. Set aside specific times for studying.
- It is better to study for a few minutes every day than to pack it all into a couple of hours once a week.
- Think about times during the day when you have to wait or your time is not fully used (for example on the way to or from work or waiting for an appointment). You can use these times to go over material (listening to cassettes in the car, learning words or reading in the bus, at the doctor's, etc).
- A change is as good as a rest: it is better, for example, to spend a few minutes every day on vocabulary, then a bit on grammar and then perhaps some time on a dialogue than it is to only do grammar one day and just dialogues the next.
- When you learn something before you go to bed and then review it the next morning, you remember it even better. Try it out and see if it works.

Monday	8–8:30 pm German (new words)
Tuesday	7:30–9 pm German class
Wednesday	9–9:45 pm German (homework: new grammar)
Thurday	7:30–9 pm German class
Friday	7–7:45 pm Read vocabulary cards
Saturday	10–11 am Homework, practise dialogues with cassettes
Sunday	Hear nothing! See nothing! Learn nothing!

8 Techniques for learning vocabulary

In sections 9–14 we have put together tips and techniques that can help you to learn new words more easily. Try them out and also think about learning with all your senses!

9 Linking new structures and words to language already known

Find connections between words and expressions you want to learn and ones you know.

1 When you are learning new words, think about whether or not you know any other words from the same word family. For example, when you find the verb lehren (to teach) in a text and you relate it to the noun Lehrer (teacher), it is much easier to remember.

2 Make comparisons – either in German or with your language. In German there are a lot of words that are similar to words in other languages, for example: German: Kopie, English: copy, Italian: copia, French: copie, Polish: kopia.

▶ Do you recognize any of the following words from somewhere else?
Politik, Computer, Radio, Kindergarten, Gitarre, Theater, Konferenz, Kultur

10 Organizing and grouping vocabulary

10.1 Grouping words according to similarities and opposites

When you have a new word to learn, think of whether or not you already know any other words with a similar meaning. For example you can learn the word heiß with warm or Mädchen with Frau. You can also put words that show a difference in degree together, for example kalt – warm – heiß or gehen – laufen – rennen. If you already know a word with the opposite meaning, you can learn pairs of opposites, for example: Junge – Mädchen, heiß – kalt, groß – klein.

10.2 Forming word families

The German language contains a lot of words that are formed from other words and compound words. Knowing this can help you to learn them, for example: arbeiten – die Arbeit – der Arbeiter – die Arbeitslosigkeit – die Arbeitzeit …

10.3 Grouping according to subject

Country – Nationality – Language: Deutschland – Deutsche/r – Deutsch
Family: Großvater – Großmutter – Vater – Mutter – Sohn – Tochter …

10.4 Making word networks

For example a skier, who often goes skiing in Austria, might have the following associations with the word Berg:

▶ Pick a topic that interests you. Write down ten words that are connected to this topic and look up the German words in the dictionary. Make a network. Learn the words.

10.5 Finding your own personal way of learning words

Group words according to criteria that have a special meaning for you personally and, therefore, will enable you to learn them more easily. For example you may want to group fruits or vegetables according to colour, or objects that you find around the house according to whether you can "hear" them or "smell" them. Or you may want to group words by how they sound, for example rhyming words or words that start or end with the same letter, and then use them in sentences.

11 Learning words in context

11.1 Using an example sentence

Kassette   Hören Sie die Kassette.
heißen   Ich heiße Petra.

11.2 Learning a number of words in one sentence

essen, trinken, Schnitzel, Bier:
Ich esse am liebsten Schnitzel und trinke Bier.

Telefonauskunft, Telefonnummer, Vorwahl: Die Telefonauskunft nennt die Telefonnummer und die Vorwahl.

11.3 Writing texts from a network

Ich gehe ins Restaurant. Die Kellnerin bringt die Speisekarte. Ich habe Hunger. Ich bestelle ein Schnitzel mit Pommes frites und Salat und ein Glas Bier. Die Kellnerin bringt die Rechnung. Ich bezahle und gebe zwei Mark Trinkgeld.

11.4 Sorting words according to personal likes and dislikes

Likes
Schnitzel
Äpfel
Sommer
Meer
rote Socken

Dislikes
Suppe
Birnen
Winter
Großstädte
blaue Socken

12 Words and pictures

12.1 Linking words and pictures

The articles present a problem for learners of German because there are three of them: der, das and die. In most other languages instead of three articles there are just one or two or often none at all. The articles represent masculine (der), neutral (das) and feminine (die). Now think up a picture of something that for you is typically masculine, let's say a lion (der Löwe). Then draw a picture that shows some kind of a relationship between this lion and all the words that use the article der. Do the same thing with das and die. In **euro**lingua **Deutsch** we have drawn a house (das Haus) and a fairy (die Fee) beside the lion as suggestions. But it is more important that you choose pictures that work for you.

12.2 Drawing pictures to illustrate the meanings of words

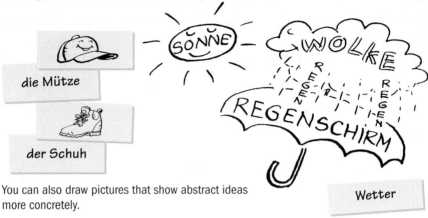

die Mütze

der Schuh

You can also draw pictures that show abstract ideas more concretely.

12.3 Making up stories from pictures

It can be fun to think up whole stories from what you see in a picture and either tell them or write them down. Start with a picture that you find interesting, possibly out of a magazine. If there are people in the picture, make up characteristics (name, age, where they live, job, likes, dislikes, what they do in their free time, holiday trips, plans for the future ...) – your imagination need have no limits!

13 Acting out words

- Don't be afraid to move a bit when you are learning. Sometimes it may help to learn words and expressions the way you would a scene from a play.
- Mime the meaning of the word you are learning and say it out loud.
- With certain words and expressions it is particularly helpful to use appropriate gestures, for example when you are explaining to someone how to get somewhere.

14 Using flash cards

Write the words on file cards. Mark where the stress is. Make notes about grammar
points. Add examples.

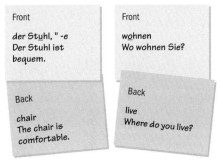

Front

der St_u_hl, " -e
Der Stuhl ist
bequem.

Front

w_o_hnen
Wo wohnen Sie?

Front

g_u_t – b_e_sser –
am b_e_sten
Schnitzel ist besser
als Hamburger.

Front

m_i_t (+D)
Ich lebe mit meinem
Freund zusammen.

Back

chair
The chair is
comfortable.

Back

live
Where do you live?

On the back put any translations and
comments in your own language. On the
left there are two examples if your mother
tongue is English.

It is a good idea to make a card index with three compartments.
Keep cards with new words in the **first compartment**. You can organize these words any
way you like: according to the type of word, topics, "easy" or "difficult" words, etc.
Put the words you have already learnt once in the **second compartment**. In the **third
compartment** put the words you are already sure of. You can
organize the third compartment alphabetically.
When you are going over words always start with the first
compartment. Whenever you think you know a word put it in
the second compartment. Next check a few words in the second
compartment to see if you still know them. If you do, put them in the third compartment.
Every once in a while pull a few cards from the third compartment and see if you really
do remember the words. If you don't, put them back in the second compartment.

▶ Look at the card index and file cards on pages 18–19 in the course book, volume 1.

15 Ways of learning grammar

The grammar sections in **eurolingua** are designed to familiarize you with the rules of the
German language and to make them easier to understand. Grammar rules aren't "laws",
but rather general descriptions that can help us to understand how the "language" works.
But of course language is much more than just grammar.
Look at grammar rules as tools that help you to express your thoughts in German. The
goal is to make yourself understood. Making mistakes is an important part of the learning process. And after a while you will find you make fewer mistakes.

There are a lot of different ways to make grammar rules easier to remember.

15.1 Working out the rules on your own

You remember a rule much better if you work it out for yourself. That is why **eurolingua** often gives you the chance to discover the grammatical regularities and to come up with the rules yourself.

▶ Now take a look at pages 20–21 in the course book, volume 1.

It is best to find your own way of remembering rules. Try making up sentences or rhymes to help you remember. Here is an example for prepositions that use the dative:

Von Ausbeimit nach Vonseitzu
fährst immer mit dem Dativ du.

15.2 Learning grammatical terms and comparing structures

Once you know what grammatical terms such as infinitive, verb, noun and adjective mean, you will be able to understand the explanations in the grammar sections better – which in turn will make learning easier.

Sometimes it may be helpful to compare German structures with those in your own language or with another foreign language that you already speak. When you sit down and compare German with English you will soon find that there are a lot of differences such as the word order in sentences:

English: Can you phone me at home tomorrow?
German: Kannst du mich morgen zu Hause anrufen?

Try not to translate word for word, but rather try to develop a feel for the German language itself.

15.3 Learning keywords

There are certain keywords that you can learn so that you remember that you have to use a special grammar rule when you see them. There is an example in section 15.1 of a rhyme you can use to help remember which prepositions always use the dative.

15.4 Visualization and drawing diagrams

Diagrams and drawings can also help you to remember grammar rules. Here is an example of how you can make the word order in German sentences clearer.

Show verbs like this: ⬭   Show subjects like this: ▭

| Ich | (arbeite) | zu Hause. |

| Morgen | (arbeite) | ich | nicht. |

| (Arbeiten) | Sie | bei Siemens? |

15.5 Tell someone else

Explain the grammar rules that you already understand to someone else. When you do this, it helps you to understand them better yourself. Teaching is a very good way of learning things better yourself.

16 Practising grammar

Often you will notice that even though you know a grammar rule very well, when you open your mouth to say something, you make the same old mistake.
Don't worry about it, it is completely normal. Some forms just take longer to master than others. The important thing is to practise as much as possible and to correct yourself when you see you have made a mistake. After a while the rule will become second nature and you will use it automatically without even having to think about it.

Even if you are not living in a German-speaking country, you should be able to find German texts (advertising, instructions, classified ads, Internet, etc). Look more closely at the texts and try to discover the grammar points you already know. Every once in a while buy a German-language newspaper or magazine and first of all see if you can understand the headlines, captions and shorter articles.

Now and then try to consciously listen more closely when you or someone else is speaking. Concentrate on one particular problem you may have with grammar, ie word order, prepositions, etc. You may be able to find mistakes you make yourself and little by little correct them.

17 Making up your own exercises and exchanging them

Make up your own vocabulary and grammar exercises to check your progress. You can also make up tests for different sections in the course book and exchange them with other students in your class. Start a file for exercises and tests and every now and then go back and do them again. In the next sections we have put together a number of different kinds of exercises that can be useful and interesting.

17.1 Rhymes

Put together pairs of words that rhyme and then write short poems which you can then read out loud for others.

Welt – Geld
kaufen – laufen

Ton – Telefon
leise – heiße

In dieser Welt
regiert das Geld.
Willst du was kaufen,
musst du laufen.

Ich hör den Ton
vom Telefon.
Es tutet laut und leise
und fragt mich, wie ich heiße.

17.2 Word puzzles

Make up a word puzzle. If possible, pick out words that are connected to the same theme (ie family members, furniture, days of the week, months and seasons, food, buildings, etc) or that are the same kind of word (part of speech) (verbs, adjectives, nouns, etc). Here are examples of a simple crossword puzzle and a puzzle where you have to find hidden words.

1 Crossword puzzle

1. Er hat Kinder. Er ist V…
2. Sie hat Kinder. Sie ist M…
3. Sohn von 1 sagt: „Die 6 des Bruders vom meinem 1 ist meine C…"
4. Der Sohn des Sohnes von 1: E…
5. Sohn von 1 sagt: „Der Bruder von 3 ist mein C…"
6. Sie ist die T… von 1 + 2.

```
              F
1. □ □ A □ □ □
      2. □ M □ □ □ □
3. □ □ □ □ I □ □
4. □ □ □ □ L □
5. □ □ □ □ I □ □
6. □ □ □ □ □ E □
```

2 Hidden words

There are ten words that are connected with "eating" (Essen) in this puzzle.

In a puzzle like this you can also hide whole sentences that someone else has to find.

V	K	U	C	H	E	N	N	W	F	H	Y	T
T	E	I	S	B	E	C	H	E	R	Y	M	T
F	Z	W	Z	E	S	A	N	D	W	I	C	H
H	N	E	Q	S	H	F	E	B	I	E	R	H
B	H	I	Y	P	T	R	I	N	K	E	N	T
M	I	N	E	R	A	L	W	A	S	S	E	R
U	A	P	F	E	L	S	A	F	T	S	X	O
M	O	L	V	S	F	H	I	I	N	E	X	N
J	R	M	K	S	R	K	B	R	O	N	U	W
S	F	E	I	O	X	W	Y	R	C	P	F	G

▶ You can probably come up with other kinds of puzzles that you can use for learning German.

17.3 Odd word out

Put together words where one word doesn't belong. Then working with others, read each group of words out loud. The others then say which word doesn't belong and write it down.
Afterwards, possibly working with a partner, try to make up a text using all of the words that didn't belong. The text should be as short as possible and it is all right if it is funny or absurd.

Lehrer – Bedienung – Sekretärin – Restaurant
lesen – schreiben – hören – bestellen
italienisch – deutsch – französisch – bayrisch
laufen – gehen – rennen – fliegen

Wir fliegen in ein bayrisches Restaurant nach München und bestellen dort Schnitzel mit Pommes frites und Salat.

17.4 Pictures and drawings

Some groups of words lend themselves to learning using pictures. You can use illustrations from books or magazines, etc.

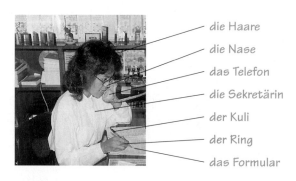

die Haare

die Nase

das Telefon

die Sekretärin

der Kuli

der Ring

das Formular

17.5 Fill in the gaps

Copy sentences from the course book and leave gaps. Some examples of gaps you can leave are:	– new words – every fifth, sixth or seventh word – all the verbs, adjectives or prepositions – all possessives – half of every word

You can include the words that have to be filled in, in the wrong order above or below the exercise. Or you can give a hint for each gap (eg the translation, a word with a similar meaning, the opposite, etc). Wait a few days and try to fill in the gaps yourself. Exchange the fill in the gap exercises with other students in your class. Here are three different examples from one text:

Der Text:
Klaus Meier kommt aus Eisenach. Er arbeitet bei Opel. Er sagt: „Ich fahre jedes Jahr drei Wochen nach Österreich. Ich habe sechs Wochen Urlaub im Jahr. Meine Freundin Petra und ich lieben die Berge."

12 Wörter fehlen:
jedes / bei / aus / Ich / ich / Er / die / nach / Meine / Er / Ich / im
Klaus Meier kommt ____ Eisenach. ____ arbeitet ____ Opel. ____ sagt: „____ fahre ____ Jahr drei Wochen ____ Österreich. ____ habe sechs Wochen Urlaub ____ Jahr. ____ Freundin Petra und ____ lieben ____ Berge. "

Bei fast jedem zweiten Wort fehlt etwa die Hälfte:
Klaus Me____ kommt a____ Eisenach. Er arbe____ bei Op____. Er sa____: „Ich fa____ jedes Ja____ drei Woc____ nach Öster____. Ich ha____ sechs Woc____ Urlaub im Ja____. Meine Freu____ Petra u____ ich lie____ die Be____."

Alle Vokale fehlen:
Kl__s M__r k_mmt __s __s_n_ch. _r _rb__t_t b__ _p_l. _r s_gt: „_ch f_hr_ j_d_s J_hr dr__ W_ch_n n_ch _st_rr__ch. _ch h_b_ s_chs W_ch_n _rl__b _m J_hr. M__n_ Fr__nd_n P_tr_ _nd _ch l__b_n d__ B_rg_."

If you use a computer, you can take the same text and make up a lot of different exercises without having to retype the text each time. Just type in the text once and save the original. Then make a copy and work with the copy. For each exercise use a new copy. After a while you will have a file full of exercises that you can call up whenever you want to rewiew something.

17.6 Jumbled texts, sentences and dialogues

Write out different parts of a sentence or of a whole text on strips of paper and mix them up. Then try to put them back in order.

On your computer you can sort the words from a sentence or a text alphabetically.

In the same way, you can also jumble the sentences from a dialogue.

One possibility is to concentrate on the role of one of the speakers which you can copy – in the wrong order, of course – below the text.

Julian: Hallo, Julian, wie geht's?
Norma:
Julian: Jetzt sehr gut. Was nimmst du? Trinkst du was?
Norma:
Julian: Einen Campari mit Orangensaft. Du auch?
Norma:
Julian: Möchtest du auch was essen?
Norma:
...

a) Das kenne ich nicht, aber o.k., ich probiere es.
b) Ja, gerne – äh – was trinkst du?
c) Ja, ich hab einen Bärenhunger. Was gibt es denn?
d) Danke, gut, und dir?

17.7 Keywords from a dialogue

Choose a dialogue or part of a dialogue from the course book (eg volume 1, p 46). Copy the parts of one of the speakers and just put in keywords for the other speaker's part. Then, using the keywords, try to reconstruct the conversation and read it out loud a couple of times.

Susi: (Portugal?)
Norma: Nein, aus Angola.
Susi: (was / machen in Berlin?)
Norma: Ich arbeite bei der Botschaft. Was macht ihr?
Susi: (Julian – Mechaniker / ich – Sekretärin)
...

Instead of using a written dialogue, you could also choose a listening dialogue from the cassette. Write down keywords for each of the speakers in the dialogue. Then try to "replay" the whole conversation. For longer dialogues you can choose one part of the conversation. You can then use the tapescripts (eg volume 1, pp 211–234) to check how well you did.

18 Learner's diary

Another good idea is to start a Learner's diary and to write anything you want in it, for example:
– your experiences (in class / when studying), your thoughts, your wishes;
– a few texts or dialogues;
– example sentences for new or especially difficult grammatical structures and words;
– word networks or words that you think of that are connected with specific topics;
– useful expressions or idioms;
– German words, sentences or short texts that you come across, eg from advertising, on food packaging, in the newspaper ...;
– songs or poems that you like;
– short stories or poetry that you write yourself.

The possibilities are limitless.

Montag, 29. Februar
Heute haben wir im Kurs Texte geschrieben. Es hat Spaß gemacht.
Akkusativ – Dativ: Noch sehr schwierig für mich!

Sonntag, 17. März
Ich habe zum ersten Mal auf Deutsch geträumt. Ich war mit Fabiane im Kino. Dann waren wir essen. Wir haben nur Deutsch gesprochen.
Es war toll!

19 Keeping track of progress in learning

Set up a table – maybe at the back of your diary – where you can keep track of your progress in learning German. Write down what you have done to improve your German, which methods you have used and how you would assess the results.

Datum	Wo?	Was?	leicht/schwierig?	Kommentar
1. März	zu Hause	Perfekt	Vergangenheit leichter als auf Englisch	Ich kann fast alle Partizip-II-Formen.
3. März	im Auto	Hörtext: M. Güler	viele neue Wörter	Geht super!

20 Listening comprehension

Hearing a language is the first step to speaking a language. But of course you cannot just hear something passively, you also have to listen actively in order to understand what is being said. Facial expressions and gestures also help you to understand what a person is saying. That is why it is easier to understand people on TV than it is on the radio. In order to practise listening comprehension you will often work with recordings that are part of the **eurolingua** course. It is normal not to understand every word the first time you hear a recording. Concentrate on the content, not on the words. At first, try to figure out what topic is being dealt with and to pick out a few pieces of information. Don't be afraid to make guesses where you are not sure. Listen to a recording two or three times and each time gather more information. And above all, don't reach for the tapescript right away because it all seems so difficult. Each time you listen you will understand a bit more.

Here are some tips to help practise listening comprehension:

20.1 Before listening to the recording

Think about the following questions:

1 What do I already know about the situation?

2 Why am I listening to something?
– Do I want some particular information (eg to know what the weather will be like)?
– Am I more interested in a getting a general overview (eg listening to the news)?
– Do I have to take down detailed notes (eg to give someone a telephone message)?

3 What am I about to listen to?
– How many people will be speaking?
– Who is talking to who?
– When and where is the conversation taking place?
– What are they talking about?

4 Can I predict what I am going to hear?
In a lot of cases you can guess what you are going to hear and so you can make certain preparations as far as special language goes. Take the case where you want to reserve a table in a restaurant. Even before you reach for the receiver, you can be fairly sure what you will be asked (Für wie viele Personen ist der Tisch? Tag und Uhrzeit? Ihr Name?). The more you can "get into" the listening situation before it even starts, the better you will be able to understand what is being said. For example, you can even prepare yourself for listening to the news on the radio or watching it on TV if you take a look at the headlines in the daily newspaper first.

20.2   **While you are listening**

1 Watch for repetitions and signals
In the spoken language the same thing will often be said more than once in a slightly different way. Listen for signals that let you know the speaker is going to explain something in more detail, for example expressions such as zum Beispiel or mit anderen Worten. Other signals to watch for are expressions that the speaker uses to introduce a certain kind of thought: Ich glaube, dass ... (= the person is expressing his opinion or making a guess) or Mach doch ... (= the person is giving advice), etc.

2 Watch for words that are easy to understand
Listen for the following kinds of words that are often easy to pick out in a spoken text:
– names of people and places,
– words and expressions that are similar to those in your mother tongue,
– numbers.

3 Guess the meaning of new words from their context
Some of the words you hear are not as important as others. With adjectives, for example, it is often enough to understand whether they have a positive or negative meaning. Try to guess the meanings of the two adjectives hässlich and hervorragend from the context.

> Das Restaurant liegt in einem hässlichen Teil von Mannheim, umgeben von Fabriken und Lagerhäusern. Aber das Essen ist hervorragend. Besonders die Vorspeisen und die Fischgerichte schmecken sehr gut.

4 Watch for non-verbal signals
When you can see the person who is speaking, watch his or her facial expressions and gestures closely. On TV the graphics and pictures can also help you to understand.

5 Don't be afraid to ask
When you are having a conversation with someone, don't hesitate to ask about things you don't understand or if you are not sure you have understood properly. Feel free to ask the person you are talking to if they could please repeat what they said or if they could speak more slowly.

21   Practising listening comprehension

21.1   Recording TV and radio broadcasts

Make recordings of broadcasts using a video recorder or cassette recorder so that you can play them back over and over again. Make sure you know why you are listening. Would you like to:
– understand the general context?
– pick out specific information from a spoken text?
– understand every word?

To practise understanding the general context, try watching German-language films or TV programmes. Choose something you have already seen and enjoyed. Give yourself a pat on the back everytime you understand something. Think positively!

She is concentrating on what she already knows.   He is concentrating on the things he doesn't know.

If you are interested in understanding a spoken text in detail, choose something that is designed for your learning level. There are numerous listening cassettes and videos produced specially for students learning German.

To train your listening comprehension in different situations, you can choose the appropriate techniques from the following. You can also ask your teacher for tips!

21.2 Recognizing what kind of a broadcast you are listening to

Tune into different German-language radio stations. Try to find out as quickly as possible what kind of a broadcast you are listening to (eg news, special report, interview, radio drama, commercial, etc). Check to see if you were right by listening a bit longer or looking it up in the radio programme schedule in the newspaper.

21.3 Listening for particular information

Choose a radio or TV broadcast that you find interesting. Before you listen to it or watch it, write down a question, eg:
– weather: What will the weather be like in Berlin tomorrow?
– news: Has anything happened in my country?
Pay attention to names of places and people, international words and expressions and numbers. While you are listening, write down key words which are connected with your question. This way it can even be fun to listen to texts that are above your present level.

21.4 Reconstructing a listening text word for word

Pick out a recording from **eurolingua Deutsch**. While you are listening to it jot down notes. Listen to the recording again and make more notes. In this way you can fill in more details each time you listen to it until you have reconstucted the whole text word for word.

22 Speaking

To be able to speak a foreign langage, you need a lot of practice because when you are speaking, you don't really have a lot of time to think about what you want to say. It helps to realize that you make mistakes in your own language as well, eg starting sentences twice, repeating yourself or not finishing sentences. Usually the person you are speaking to understands what you are saying anyway. That is because the situation is clear or the context helps. And if not, you can always ask about things you don't understand. There are a lot of different "standard situations" in communication and you can prepare yourself for the ones you will probably be needing, as in the example of reserving a table. (→ 📖 A 20.1/4)

22.1 Before you start speaking

Go through a conversation in your head. before you start talking to someone. Which words and expressions will you probably need? It helps to be clear about what the other person already knows and what they expect from you. For example, when you want to buy

a piece of clothing, the questions you will have to ask and the information you will have to supply will be different from when you want to order a meal in a restaurant.
Make up lists of expressions and vocabulary that you need for the "standard situations" that are most important for you.

22.2 While you are speaking

1 Simple stuctures
Avoid long sentences and complex structures. The simpler and shorter, the better! When you are speaking, try to think in German and not in your mother tongue. At first it won't be very easy, but you will find that after a while, you will be able to speak longer and longer passages "automatically" without having to "plan" them in your own language first.

2 Intonation
Pay attention to the intonation. Speak loudly and clearly. Try to imitate the way native German speakers talk. Don't be afraid to exaggerate a little. Don't worry if your pronunciation is not "perfect". Very few people ever manage to speak a foreign language completely without an accent. The most important thing is that people understand you.

3 Concentrate on the content
Don't worry that you might possibly make a grammatical error. If someone were to ask you on the street: Where station, please?, you would understand the question and be able to give directions without any problem. It would, of course, be a different story if the person were to mix up station and airport.

4 Use your hands and feet
Use facial expressions and gestures when you cannot think of a word or expression. You can also try to use other words to describe the idea you are trying to get across.

Möchten Sie eine Zeitung kaufen?
Suchen Sie einen Zeitungsladen?

Ich suche – Laden, äh, also – ich brauche – äh – hm – wie sagt man das auf Deutsch – lesen – Nachrichten …

Ja, danke! Ich suche einen Zeitungsladen.

5 The reactions of the person you are talking to
Watch the other person's reactions. Have they understood what you said? Don't be afraid to keep on checking with questions like: Verstehen Sie, was ich meine? (Do you understand what I mean?) If you cannot think of a word you need, try to say it using other words.

23.1   Roleplaying

Sometimes you will be asked to do roleplays, in other words, to act out an everyday situation as "true-to-life" as possible.
Try as hard as you can to get into the role
of the person you are playing and to act as
realistically as possible. If the situation
calls for it, stand up and move about the
classroom. If you don't know all of the
expressions you need by heart, write down
a few key phrases on a piece of paper.

23.2   Reading out loud

Pick out texts you like and read them out loud. If you choose a text from the course book
with a recording, listen to the recording first and then try to imitate the intonation.

23.3   Learning texts by heart

Choose a text you like (eg a dialogue or a poem) and learn it by heart. If it happens to be
a listening text from **eurolingua**, one way you can do it is as follows:

– Listen to the text and then repeat the sentences. Pay attention to the intonation. Mark
  any possible places where you have difficulty (stress in words or in the sentences).
– Read the text out loud several times.
– Play the recording again and stop it now and again and try to continue on your own.

Do you like singing? If so, you can learn German songs by heart and sing them.
eurolingua Deutsch supplies you with a whole series of songs. A lot of German CDs
include the printed lyrics. Pick out a song that you also have the lyrics to and sing along.

23.4 Planning dialogues

Every now and then pick a situation that you have already dealt with in class (eg reserving a hotel room by telephone) and jot down all of the expressions and words that are connected with it that you can still remember. Check yourself by looking the situation up in the course book or in Part B in the Learner's Handbook.

23.5 Dialogue graphics

In **euro**lingua **Deutsch** you will often find graphics representing dialogues. They sketch out the sequence of the dialogue, but you have to figure out what you have to say. Design dialogue graphics yourself and exchange them in class.

▶ Take a look at the dialogue graphics in the course book, volume 1 on pages 12 (3.1), 46 (1.8) and 59 (2.2).

23.6 Collecting useful expressions

Put together a card index of useful expressions. You organize it the same way as the one for vocabulary. In the third compartment you can arrange the expressions according to topic or situation (greeting people, shopping for food, clothes or shoes, etc). For different topics you can also look at the **Language in Use** column in the table of contents in the course book. Here are a few possibilities for making your own flash cards, eg on the subject of Einkaufen.

1

Front: what you intend to say in German   Back: the German expression

nach dem Preis fragen	Wie viel kosten die Kirschen?

2

Front: what you intend to say in German and the expression in German

Back: the corresponding response in German

Verkäufer fragt, ob man noch etwas möchte: – Noch etwas?	+ Ja, ich hätte gerne noch ein Pfund Bananen. + Nein, danke. Das ist alles.

23.7 Practising with a cassette recorder

With a cassette recorder, record expressions that are important for you in specific situations, eg when you are shopping or involved in a discussion. Repeat them more than once onto the cassette. Then you can listen to them when you are driving, or at home when you are cooking or before you go to sleep, etc.

Ich hätte gern ein Pfund Tomaten.

Another thing you can do is to record one of the speakers from a dialogue in the book, leaving space for the response of the other speaker. Then rewind and play the recording back, taking the role of the second speaker. For a longer dialogue you can note down keywords for your role to help you out.

23.8 Contact with German speakers

Maybe you know some native German speakers who you see regularly and can speak German to. Another ideal situation is to find a native German speaker who wants to learn your language. Then you can get together regularly for a "language exchange". Try contacting someone through a classified ad in your local paper or in the Internet. (→ 📖 A 26.3)

24 Reading comprehension

People learning foreign languages are often unhappy when they don't understand every word in a text. Either they give up or they spend a lot of time looking up words in the dictionary that they don't really need in order to be able to understand the text. In most cases it is not important to understand every single word to get the information you need from a text.
There are a lot of different ways of reading a text. You can skim for particular information or read everything word for word. How you read a text at any given time depends on what kind of a text you are reading and what your interests are.

▶ Pay attention to how you read in your own language. How do you read the daily paper? A novel? How about recipes?

1 Reading globaly
When you want to get a general picture of what is happening in the world you "skim" the corresponding articles in the paper. In this case details do not matter as much as finding out the most important information.

2 Selective reading

If you are interested in finding out if there is a detective film or drama on TV in the evening, you look for that information specifically. Descriptions of other programmes don't interest you at all.

19.50 Sportschau-Telegr. 9-834-208
20.00 Tagesschau 88-463
20.15 Tatort: Eulenburg
FILM Krimi, BRD/A/CH '96 2-180-227
Regie: Sylvia Hoffman.
Der Geschäftsmann Bohländer wird erschossen. Als Kommissar Brinkmann (Karl-Heinz von Hassel) seine junge Kollegin Alice Bothe von dem Fall abziehen muß, ermittelt sie auf eigene Faust → S. 74

heute:
der Meere → **S. 68**
20.15 Laß Dich überraschen
TIP Die Show voller 2-188-869
Emotionen. Moderator Thomas Ohrner erfüllt wieder einigen Zuschauern ihre sehnlichsten Herzenswünsche, die ihm von netten Freunden und Verwandten anvertraut wurden → **S. 69**
21.45 Lukas 260-192
TIP Comedyserie

tiefen Steilhang hinab
20.15 Ein verrücktes Paar –
Alt verkracht und frisch
verliebt 3-548-666
FILM Komödie, USA 1993
Regie: Donald Petrie.
Die Witwer John Gustafson (Jack Lemmon) und Max Goldman (Walter Matthau) machen sich mit niederträchtigen Beleidigungen und fiesen Streichen gegenseitig das

FC Hansa Rostock → **S. 70**
20.15 Der Bulle von Tölz:
FILM **Waidmanns Zank**
TV-Krimi, BRD 1996 2-846-685
Regie: Walter Bannert.
Der Jäger Burger beschuldigt den Wirt Schaller der Wilderei Al...

Der Programmauszug folgt noch der alten Rechtschreibnorm.

3 Reading word for word

When you are using a recipe to cook supper, you have to read the instructions very precisely. In this case every word is important. The same thing is true for the instructions you get at work or in users' manuals, for example. But it is also important when you are reading poetry.

The first thing to think about whenever you read something is: Why? (How you read texts in the course book is guided by the reading tasks.) When you know why you are reading something, you can then choose the reading technique that is appropriate.

25   What should I watch out for when I am reading?

25.1   Before reading

Think about:

1 Where is the text from (a letter, newspaper, brochure, novel, conversation, instruction manual, etc)?

2 What topic is being dealt with in the text?

3 What kind of readership is being addressed (general public, experts, children, etc)?

4 With what intentions was the text written (entertainment, information, personal opinion, etc)?

Hotel Ibis Dresden Lilienstein
306 Zimmer, Dusche, WC, Telefon, Radio, Satelliten-TV. Nichtraucheretagen. Restaurant, Bar. Frühstücksbuffet.
Prager Straße
zentrale Lage, direkt in der Fußgängerzone

Hotel Ibis Dresden Lilienstein

5 Am I more interested in finding specific information (eg in the telephone book), in getting a general picture (eg from the newspaper) or in reading everything very precisely, for example because I have to take notes (eg from a travel brochure)?

Often titles, subtitles, illustrations (pictures, photos) with captions give a hint about the topic and structure of the text. Different ways in which words are marked in the text can also help you to understand it. In some texts you will find certain words printed in CAPITALS, *italics*, **bold** or <u>underlined</u>. These are usually keywords, words that the author thought were important.

Wer eine Sonnenfinsternis beobachtet, muss die Augen schützen.

25.2   While reading

1 How the text is organized can help you to orientate yourself. Usually texts are divided into paragraghs and each paragraph contains a main thought or idea. Try to understand what they are.

2 Don't reach for your dictionary the minute you find a word you don't understand. First of all try to guess the meaning of the word yourself. There are different strategies for doing this.

25.3   Strategies for finding out the meanings of new words

1 Maybe there are words that look similar in your language or another language you know. In particular in the areas of politics, science, academics and the media there are a lot of so called "international words". Compare the following:

German	English	French	Polish
Präsident	president	président	prezydent
Politik	politics	politique	polityka

2 Maybe you can figure out the meaning of the word by looking at the different parts the word is made up of. Is the unknown word a compound word? German has a lot of words put together from two or more shorter words. When you already know the words Sonne and Blume, it is easy enough to figure out what the compound word Sonnenblume means.

3 Maybe the new word is a derivative of a word you already know. German has very special patterns of how words are derived from other words. Quite likely, you would understand the following German words without any problem even if you had never heard them or seen them before:

Schönheit = schön + heit
unglücklich = un + Glück + lich
Lernerhandbuch = Lerner + Hand + Buch

4 What kind of word (part of speech) is the new word? Is it a noun, verb or adjective? Usually you can tell by the context. In German the fact that all nouns are capitalized is an additional help.

In the following three sentences we have put in a nonsense word, "waggle". Can you tell what type of word (part of speech) it represents in each of the three sentences?

Ich habe ein Waggle. Mein Auto ist waggle. Es waggelt über 200 km/h.

5 Maybe you can guess the meaning of the unknown word from the context. Suppose you see the following sentence:

Bernard schenkt Claudine rote Nesor zu ihrem Geburtstag. (Bernard gives Claudine red Nesor for her birthday.)

You don't know the word Nesor. However you do know that it has to be a noun because it comes after an adjective and is capitalized. So Nesor stands for a thing that can be red and that a person would give someone else for their birthday. Now look more closely at the context. The next sentence is: Sie stellt sie in eine Vase. (She puts them in a vase.) You can assume that Nesor must be some kind of flowers. When you are reading, this should be enough information and you go on. You have understood the meaning of the sentence. Of course if you especially love flowers, you may want to find out exactly what kind of flowers are meant. Then you can look it up in the dictionary. (But you won't find the word Nesor in the dictionary. Just read it backwards.)

26 Practising reading comprehension

Reading is a wonderful way of developing your feeling for the language as it helps you to enlarge your vocabulary and get used to the grammatical patterns of the language. Read the same things in German that you like reading in your own language. The following tips may help you choose something to read.

26.1 Magazines or newspapers

Thumb through newspapers or magazines and try to find out how they are put together (Where can you find what? What sections are there?).

▶ Find a short article in a German paper that you think may be interesting. Read it without using a dictionary. Make notes answering the following questions:
- What is the article about?
- Who did what?
- What happened?
- Where, when and why did it happen?

If you cannot answer any of these questions, then think about whether or not the dictionary can help you further. First of all, make a list of not more than three to five words you think may help and look them up. If you still cannot answer the questions, then try looking up a few more.

26.2 Stories and novels

Choose something that corresponds to the level of your course. In bookstores there is a variety of well-known novels and short stories that have been shortened and where the language has been simplified. Your teacher can probably help you to choose something.

26.3 Texts from the Internet

Look for forums written in German. Look for news that is of interest to you. Print it out and read it at leisure. You can use the following address as a start.

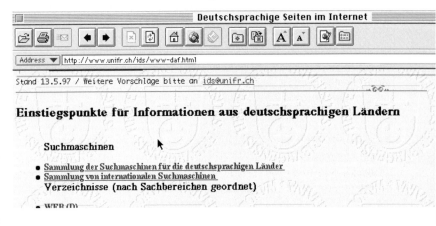

In your German course, writing serves two purposes.

1 Writing to help you learn
You write in German in order to learn the language.
– You write down words and expressions because the way the words look helps you to remember them.
– When you fill in the gaps in a text or write a short text on a particular topic, you have time to think about the correct forms and the best way to formulate your ideas in German.
– When you take notes while listening to a recording, you increase your concentration.

2 Writing to convey information
As time goes on, you will be writing more and more texts in which you want to let someone know something. Ask yourself the following questions before you start writing:
– Who is going to read what I write? (reader)
– What do I want to say? (content)
– How do I want to say it? (form)

Writing texts has to be learnt systematically. It is good to start by writing short texts, taking more time to plan them and correct them. Instead of just starting to write, you should take your time and go step by step.

27.1 Before you start writing a text

1 Brainstorming
Jot down any terms and ideas connected with the topic that come to mind (in your own language or in German).

2 Making an outline
Fill out and make additions to the points you have and put them in order. Try to keep your text as simple and clear as possible. Which points belong together?

What comes at the beginning / in the body of the text / at the end?

3 Getting together vocabulary and making up sentences
Find the important words and expressions you need for your text. Put them together in sentences or parts of sentences. Try to write as simply as possible using expressions and structures that you already know. Use your dictionary as little as possible.

27.2 While you are writing

Now write the complete text. Use the language elements that you have gathered. Join the sentences and parts of sentences with words such as und, aber, weil, denn, trotzdem, etc or with expressions such as einerseits – anderseits, nicht nur … sondern auch, etc.
Don't rush yourself. At the beginning take your time and write slowly.

27.3 After writing

1 Proofread your text
Read your text through more than once. Each time you read it, concentrate on just one well-defined problem, such as:

– Is the word order right? (Aussagesätze, W-Fragen, Ja/Nein-Fragen, Nebensätze)
– Do the verb forms agree (person, tense)?
– Do the adjective and noun endings agree (plural, case)?
– Are the sentences logically connected?
– Are the nouns all capitalized?

If you are not sure, check in the Learner's Handbook or in a dictionary. Exchange your work with other students in your class whenever possible.

2 Statistics: Try to find out where you make the most mistakes. When you are proofreading, concentrate on these kinds of mistakes until you notice you are making fewer of them.

Fehlerstatistik	Korrekturen/Beispiele
1. Wortstellung: 3 Fehler	Ich (wohne) in Seckenheim.
2. Verbformen: 2 Fehler	Mein Freund heißt Tom.
3. Adjektivendungen: 2 Fehler	Er hat eine schöne Wohnung.
4. …	

28   Practising writing

28.1   Using texts as a pattern and making variations

For example, take a text from the course book and copy it. While you are doing this you can vary it by changing the information and fitting it to yourself. Don't try to change the text too much at the beginning. Later you will find you can become more and more creative in your variations.

▶ Read the text on page 33 in the course book, volume 1 (5.1) and vary it.

> Das ist Birsen Coban.
> Sie ist Psychologin.
> Birsen und Sedat
> sind verheiratet.
> Birsen ist aus ...
> Das liegt in der Nähe
> von ...
> ...

28.2   Text – keywords – text

Using one of the texts from the course book, write down keywords. After a few days, try to rewrite the text using the keywords.

> Boris/Barbara Becker + Sohn
> Noah – Tennisspieler – Leimen –
> München – Monaco

28.3   Chain of events

In German write down actions that you repeat everyday. This way you can enlarge your vocabulary at the same time as you are practising composing simple sentences. Divide the chains into smaller groups of three or four sentences. Here is an example:

Vom Bett zum Bus

Der Wecker klingelt.
Ich stehe nicht auf.
Der Wecker klingelt noch einmal.

Ich stehe auf.
Ich gehe ins Bad.
Ich wasche mich.
Ich putze mir die Zähne.

Ich mache Kaffee.
Ich mache mir ein Toastbrot mit
   Marmelade.

Ich hole die Zeitung aus dem
   Briefkasten.
Ich lese die Zeitung.
Ich höre die Nachrichten im Radio.
Ich höre mein Lieblingslied.

Es ist 7 Uhr 15.
Ich bin zu spät.
Ich renne zur Bushaltestelle.
Der Bus ist weg.

28.4 Pen friends

See if you can find someone who is willing to
exchange letters with you in German. Maybe
there is a German course in another city
that would like to twin up with your course.
Write short letters, postcards, greeting
cards, invitations, etc to each other.

28.5 Internet and e-mail

The electronic media offers a lot of possibilities for the exchange of ideas.
Try to establish contact with other German learners and with German-speaking people.
(→ 📖 A 26.3)

29 Dictionaries

29.1 Choosing a dictionary

A good dictionary is a great help when learning a language. For beginners it is best to get
a bilingual dictionary. Your teacher should be able to help you decide which one to buy.
Important things to bear in mind when you are choosing a good dictionary are:
− Is it the latest version?
− Is it laid out clearly?
− Does it tell you how to pronounce words?
− Does it have sections on grammatical use? (eg irregular verbs)
− Do entries include spelling changes? (eg plural forms, etc)
− Are there examples of how the words (and expressions) are used? (eg where the Ger-
  man use is different)

Later it is a very good idea to get a monolingual German dictionary. Of course, since
explanations are given only in German, you won't need one until you are a bit more
advanced.

29.2 Using a dictionary

Sit down with your dictionary and get an overview of the parts it contains and how it is
organized. Often you will find sections at the beginning or at the end that contain lists (eg
weights and measures, numbers, irregular verb forms, a short grammar, etc). It is a good
idea to check what the abbreviations and symbols that are used in the dictionary mean.

29.3 Bilingual dictionaries

Not all dictionaries are organized in the same way. Generally, for each entry, you will find information on the follollowing points:

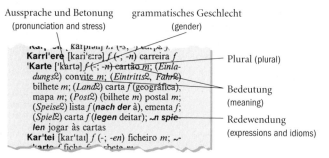

From: Langenscheidts Eurowörterbuch Portugiesisch

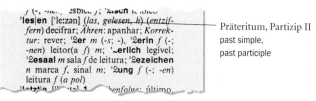

From: Langenscheidts Eurowörterbuch Portugiesisch

1 Pronunciation and stress

The phonetic spelling shows you how to pronounce the word. The stress comes on the syllable after the '. The phonetic alphabet used is explained either at the beginning or end of the book.

2 Parts of speech

Sometimes it tells you what part of speech the word is (noun, verb, adjective, adverb ...). For nouns it will show the plural forms (irregular plural form, word only used in the plural form, etc). For irregular verbs it usually shows the past simple form and the past participle.

3 Meanings

Most words have various meanings according to context. Read the whole entry through before deciding which translation is best. Then look up the entry for that word in the other section of the dictionary to make sure you really have the right word.

4 Expressions and idioms

Sometimes in an entry you will find expressions and idioms where the word is used and what it means in this case.

A monolingual dictionary will show you how a particular word is used in different contexts.

From: Langenscheidts
Großwörterbuch Deutsch
als Fremdsprache

Kar·te *die*; -, *-n*; **1** ein rechteckiges Stück aus festem (steifem) Papier, auf das man etw. schreibt ‖ -K: **Kartei- 2** e-e K. (1) (oft mit e-m aufgedruckten Foto od. Bild), die dazu dient, anderen e-e Nachricht od. e-n Gruß zu schreiben ⟨j-m aus dem Urlaub, zum Geburtstag e-e K. schicken, schreiben⟩ ‖ -K: **An- sichts-, Beileids-, Geburtstags-, Glückwunsch-, Neujahrs-, Post-, Weihnachts- 3** ≈ Eintrittskarte ⟨Karten kaufen, bestellen; Karten reservieren las- sen⟩ ‖ K-: **Karten-, -bestellung, -(vor)verkauf** ‖ -K: **Kino-, Konzert-, Theater- 4** (in Restaurants, Bars *o. ä.*) e-e Liste, auf der Speisen, Getränke *usw* u. ihre Preise stehen ⟨die K. verlangen, studieren; die K. bringen⟩ ‖ -K: **Eis-, Getränke-, Speise-,**

▶ On page 10, section 1.1 in the course book you will find the following sentence: Schreiben Sie Ihren Namen auf die Karte und stellen Sie sich vor. Which meaning of Karte seems best in this case?

1   Aids in communication

1.1   In the classroom

Asking about the meaning or use of a word ....

– Was heißt „garfo" auf Deutsch?   + Die Gabel.
– Was bedeutet „Gabel"?   + Auf Portugiesisch „garfo".
– Wie sagt man auf Deutsch:
    „Como vai, tudo bem?"   + (Man sagt:) „Hallo, wie geht's?"
– Ist „garfo" „die Gabel" auf Deutsch?   + Ja.
– Was ist der Unterschied zwischen   + Beim „Zuhören" konzentriert man
    „zuhören" und „hören"?   sich auf das „Hören" ...
– Können Sie mir ein Beispiel geben?   + „Ich höre Ihnen zu."
    „Ich höre Lärm auf der Straße."

Asking about the pronunciation or spelling of a word ....

– Wie spricht man das?
– Wo liegt bei diesem Wort die Betonung / der Wortakzent?
– Sagt man Kursleiterin oder Kursleiterin?
– Welches Wort ist in diesem Satz betont? / Wo liegt der Satzakzent?
– Spricht man den Vokal lang oder kurz?
– Sagt man Buch oder Buch?

– Können Sie das Wort bitte buchstabieren?
– Schreibt man „Kassette" mit einem oder zwei s?

Asking if something is correct ....

– Ist das richtig? / Stimmt das?
– Kann man sagen: „Mein Vorname ist Birsen"?

Saying you don't know or have forgotten something ....

– Tut mir Leid, ich weiß es nicht.
– Ich weiß nicht, was „garfo" auf Deutsch heißt.
– Ich hab das deutsche Wort für „amante" vergessen.
– Ich hab vergessen, was das auf Deutsch heißt.
– Das Wort kenne ich nicht.
– „Hausaufgaben", was ist das? Nie gehört!
– Ich hab vergessen, die Hausaufgaben zu machen.
– Ich hab mein Buch vergessen.

Saying you haven't understood something or someone ....

– Entschuldigung, ich habe Sie/dich/… nicht verstanden.
– Ich habe das noch nicht verstanden.

Asking someone to repeat something ....

– Wie bitte?
– Können Sie / Kannst du das noch mal sagen/erklären/wiederholen …?
– Wie heißt das Wort?
– Sprechen Sie / Sprich bitte etwas langsamer/lauter …
– Wiederholen Sie bitte noch einmal das letzte Wort / den letzten Satz.

1.2 Avoiding misunderstandings

Asking for an explanation when you have not understood something or are not sure if you've understood something correctly ....

– Was meinst du damit?   + Ich meine, dass …
– Stimmt es, dass das Wort „Eltern"   + Ja.
  nur im Plural vorkommt?

Checking to see if someone has understood you ....

– Haben Sie / Hast du das verstanden?
– Verstehen Sie / Verstehst du mich?
– Verstehst du, was ich meine?

1.3 In everyday situations

Asking for the right word ....

– Ich kenne das   + „Batata" heißt
  deutsche Wort   auf Deutsch
  für „batata"   „Kartoffel".
  nicht.

– Es ist aus Metall/Plastik/Holz …
– Es ist ungefähr so groß/lang/breit …
– Man braucht es zum …

Es ist ungefähr so groß.

Asking if you have not understood something or have not heard something properly ....

– Wie bitte?
– Entschuldigung, ich habe Sie nicht verstanden.
– Können Sie das bitte wiederholen?
– Was hast du gesagt?
– Können Sie bitte etwas langsamer/lauter sprechen?
  Mein Deutsch ist noch nicht so gut.

Expressing what you said in another way ....

– Was ich sagen will, ist …
– Mit anderen Worten: …
– Was ich damit meine, ist …

Letting someone know that you have understood ....

– Ich verstehe.
– Jetzt habe ich Sie / die Regel … verstanden.
– Jetzt ist mir das klar.

Checking to see if you have understood something ....

– Die Straßenbahn   + 10 Uhr 20?
  fährt um 10 Uhr 20.
– Richtig.

– Tut mir Leid, Rinder-   + Kein Rindersteak?
  steak gibt es nicht
  mehr.
– Ja.

– Hast du gesagt, du   + Nein, ins Konzert.
  willst ins Kino gehen?

2   Greetings and goodbyes

2.1   Greetings

To greet someone you can use the following expressions – depending on the time of day:

formal   *informal*

Guten Tag, Frau Graf!

Guten Tag, Herr Roth.

Tag, Rudi.

Tag, Udo.

- Guten Tag!
- Guten Morgen!
- Guten Abend!
- Grüß Gott! *(D-south)*
- Grüezi! *(CH)*

- Tag!
- Morgen!
- Abend!
- Hallo!
- Grüß dich!
- Servus! *(A)*
- Salü! *(CH)*
- Hoi! *(CH)*

When greeting someone you know, you should use their name.

- Guten Tag, Frau Müller.
- Hallo, Fabiane.

In general, when greetings adults on a formal basis, you should address them as Herr ... for men and Frau ... for women.

⚠ The form of address Fräulein (for unmarried women) is seldom used any more and is not appreciated by many women. It is much better not to use it.

In German-speaking countries it is often the custom to shake hands when greeting people – even with acquaintances and friends.
In Germany a kiss on the cheek is generally rerserved for people you know quite well, though in Switzerland it is more common.

2.2   Welcoming people in your home

- Herzlich willkommen, Frau Peterlini.
- Guten Abend, Herr Coban. Schön, dass Sie gekommen sind.
- Hallo, Ingrid, schön, dass du da bist. Komm doch rein.
- Kommen Sie doch rein und legen Sie ab.

Leaving your shoes at the door when you visit someone is not generally a custom in German-speaking countries.

2.3 Introducing yourself

When you meet someone for the first time
(eg your first day in class or at a party)
it is the custom to introduce yourself.

– Guten Morgen, ich heiße …
– Guten Tag, meine Name ist …
– Guten Abend, ich heiße …

Just saying your name is also OK:

– Brigitte Müller.

If someone does not say their name or you have not properly understood what their name is, you can ask this way:

– Wie ist Ihr Name?
– Entschuldigung, ich habe Ihren Namen nicht verstanden.

2.4 Introducing someone

In formal situations, when introducing two people to each other, you first introduce the man to the woman or the younger person to the older one.

In more informal situations you can just say the names of the people being introduced (either first name and surname or just first name) and perhaps say a little bit about them.

Hallo, Enis, das ist Nina, eine Schulfreundin von mir.
Nina, das ist Enis. Wir sind im gleichen Semester.

Hallo!

Hallo!

2.5 Asking how someone is

People who know each other often ask how the other person is.

Asking how someone is	Saying how you are and returning the question ....
– Wie geht's? – Wie geht es Ihnen? – Wie geht es dir?	☺ + Danke, (sehr) gut, und Ihnen? + Danke, prima, und dir? ☺ + Na ja, es geht. ☹ + Ach, nicht so gut.

If you don't know someone very well, the usual response is: Danke, gut.

2.6 *Sie* or *du*?

In German the Sie form has traditionally been used in formal situations. The du form was reserved for good friends and children. This is slowly changing. The du form is being used more and more for people you don't know very well. Younger people often say du to each other right away. In general, it depends on the situation, on the relationship you have to a certain person and on the individual, when and how quickly you can start to use the du form instead of the Sie form – or if the change comes at all.

⚠ When in doubt, it's probably best to use the Sie form and check for signals before changing over. Usually people will tell you if they prefer the du form.

2.7 Saying goodbye

formal	*informal*
– Auf Wiedersehen!	– Tschüs! *(D/CH)*
– Gute Nacht!	– Tschau! *(D)*
– Adieu! *(CH)*	– Ciao! *(CH)*
– Ade! *(CH)*	– Servus! *(A)*

2.8 Shaking hands / Kissing

Depending on the situation it is also customary to shake hands when saying goodbye in German-speaking countries. In Switzerland it is also quite often the case that people give each other a kiss on the cheek. In Germany and Austria this is only done with people you know quite well. (→ 📖 B 2.1)

2.9 Wishing someone well – Sending greetings

People often add the wish that all will be well or say when they will be seeing each other again:

– Alles Gute dann und bis bald!
– Bis heute Abend!
– Bis morgen!

Sometimes people add a greeting to another person both people know:

– Grüßen Sie Ihren Mann von mir.
– Grüße an Eva!

+ Danke, ich werde es ausrichten.
+ Mach ich.

3 Best wishes, congratulations, compliments

3.1 Best wishes

There are a lot of situations where it is common to wish someone the best. These wishes are often added when you say goodbye (→ 📖 B 16).

Travel ....

– Gute Reise!

End of the workday / holidays/weekend .....

– Schönen Abend!
– Schönen Urlaub! *(only D/A)*
– Schöne Ferien!
– Schönes Wochenende!

Exams/Competitions ....

– Viel Glück! / Viel Erfolg!
– Hals- und Beinbruch!
– Ich drücke Ihnen/dir die Daumen!

Gute Reise!
Schreib mal!

Danke, tschüs!

START

Hals- und Beinbruch!

Danke!

Theatre/Cinema, etc ....

– Viel Spaß!
– Viel Vergnügen!
– Gute Unterhaltung!

Guten Appetit
wünsch ich dir.

Danke,
gleichfalls.

Meals ....

– Guten Appetit!
– Mahlzeit! *(D)*
– En Guete! *(CH)*

Drinking ....

Gute
Besserung!

– Zum Wohl!
– Prost!
– Prosit!

Illness ....

– Gute Besserung!
– Baldige Besserung! *(A)*

Sneezing ....

– Gesundheit!
– Zum Wohl! *(A)*

HATSCHI

Gesundheit!

Christmas/Easter/Pentecost, etc ....

– Schöne Festtage/Feiertage!   – Frohe Weihnachten/Ostern!

New Year ....

– Alles Gute fürs neue Jahr!   – Ein gutes neues Jahr!
– Ein glückliches neues Jahr!   – Viel Glück im neuen Jahr!

Replying to special wishes ....

– Danke!
– Danke, gleichfalls!
– Das wünsche ich Ihnen/dir auch!

3.2 Congratulations and best wishes

In German-speaking countries people usually shake hands when they congratulate someone or wish them well in the case of a special day or event. People who know each other well will also kiss each other on the cheek.

Congratulating someone .... Thanking someone ....

– Herzlichen Glückwunsch zum Geburtstag!   + Danke.
– Herzliche Glückwünsche zur Hochzeit!   + Vielen Dank.
– Herzliche Glückwünsche zum Examen!   + Danke vielmals.

– Viel Glück zum Geburtstag!
– Alles Gute zur Hochzeit!

3.3 Congratulations and best wishes in writing

You can buy a printed greeting card and add your own personal message. Of course it is even more personal to write a card or letter yourself.

WIR GRATULIEREN,
WIR GRATULIEREN,
WIR GRATULIEREN!

Liebe Katja!
Wir gratulieren dir zu deinem
25. Geburtstag! Wir wünschen dir
von Herzen alles Gute und vor allem,
dass du gesund bleibst.

Oma und Großpapa

Liebe Nina, lieber Mario,
herzliche Glückwünsche zu
eurer Hochzeit und alles Gute
für euer Leben zu zweit!
Ganz liebe Grüße!

Erika

Herzliche Glückwünsche!

Alles Gute zur Hochzeit!

Letters → 📖 B 22

3.4 Compliments

A: **Deine neue Frisur
steht dir gut.**
B: **Meinst du? Danke!**

Making a compliment	Reaction
– Du siehst gut aus. Warst du in Urlaub?	+ Danke! Ich war 14 Tage am Meer.
– Der Rock steht dir gut.	+ Ja? Gefällt er dir?
– Ihre Arbeit war hervorragend.	+ Danke! Man tut, was man kann.
– Das haben Sie gut gemacht.	+ Meinen Sie?
– Das Essen schmeckt hervorragend.	+ Danke! Es freut mich, dass es dir schmeckt.
– Du kannst ja wunderbar singen/ malen/tanzen …	+ Na ja, es geht.

4 Requests, thanks, apologies

A: **Können Sie mir
bitte helfen?
Der Koffer ist
so schwer.**
B: **Aber gerne.**
A: **Vielen Dank!
Das ist nett von
Ihnen.**
B: **Nichts zu
danken.**

4.1 Requests

– Können Sie / Kannst du mir bitte helfen?
– Könnten Sie / Könntest du bitte das Fenster zumachen?
– Entschuldigung, haben Sie / hast du einen Kuli für mich?
– Bitte komm / kommen Sie morgen pünktlich.
– Rufen Sie mich / Ruf mich bitte am Wochenende an.
(→ 📖 B 8, 24, C 20.5)

4.2 Thanks

In German-speaking countries people often shake hands when thanking someone for something.

Thanking someone for something	Reaction ....
– Danke (schön) für das Geschenk.	+ Bitte (schön/sehr)!
– Danke vielmals für die Blumen.	+ Gern geschehen.
– Vielen Dank für Ihre Hilfe.	+ Nichts zu danken.
– Herzlichen Dank für die Information.	+ War mir ein Vergnügen
– Tausend Dank für deinen Tipp.	+ Ist schon o.k.

4.3 Apologies

Das macht doch nichts.

Entschuldigung!

Apology	Reaction ....
– Entschuldigung!	+ Das macht (doch) nichts.
– Verzeihung! *(D)*	+ Nicht so schlimm.
– Pardon! *(CH)*	+ Das kann passieren.
– Das tut mir (sehr) Leid!	+ Das kann ja mal vorkommen.
– Entschuldigen Sie bitte! Das wollte ich nicht!	+ Es ist ja nichts passiert.

5 Making appointments, invitations, offers

5.1 Asking about someone's plans

A: Hast du morgen / am Wochenende / ... schon was vor?
B: Bis jetzt noch nicht. Warum?

Asking about someone's plans	Reaction ....
– Was machst du heute Abend / am Samstag ...?	+ Ich hab ein paar Freunde eingeladen. Hast du auch Lust zu kommen?
– Was machst du am Wochenende?	+ Hm, ich weiß noch nicht. Hast du eine Idee?

5.2 Suggestions/Invitations

A: Haben Sie / Hast du Lust, mit mir morgen essen zu gehen?
B: Von mir aus gerne, aber ich muss morgen arbeiten.
A: Und am Samstag?
B: Das ist prima.

– Kommen Sie / Kommst du mit ins Kino?
– Wollen wir zusammen ins Theater gehen?
– Haben Sie / Hast du Lust, nach der Arbeit ein Bier trinken zu gehen?
– Wie wär's mit Kino heute Abend?

Agreeing to a suggestion or accepting an invitation ....

– Gute Idee. Ich komme mit.
– Danke, ich komme gern.
– Danke, das ist wirklich nett von Ihnen/dir.
– Ja, o.k.

Saying no to a suggestion or invitation ....

– Nein danke, ich habe heute keine Lust.
– Ich würde gern mitkommen, aber ich habe keine Zeit.
– Heute kann ich nicht. Vielleicht ein andermal.

Haben Sie Lust, mit mir etwas trinken zu gehen?

Heute kann ich nicht. Ich muss noch arbeiten.

⚠ Usually when you say no to a suggestion or an invitation, you give a short explanation why (work, time, another invitation, illness ...).

Making another suggestion ....

– Ich habe eine andere Idee. Wie wär's mit ...
– Warum gehen wir nicht lieber spazieren?
– Wie wär's mit italienisch essen?
– Lass uns was trinken, bevor wir ins Konzert gehen.
– Ich würde lieber eine Radtour machen.

5.3 Arranging the time and place you will meet

Suggesting a time and place ....

– Wir treffen uns vor dem Eingang um 7 Uhr 30.
– Wollen wir uns an der Straßenbahnhaltestelle treffen?
– Wir können uns ja eine halbe Stunde vorher im „Theatercafé" treffen.
– Ich treffe dich dann um 8 Uhr vor dem Kino.
– Ist Ihnen/dir 8 Uhr recht?
(→ 📖 B 25)

Agreeing ....

– Das ist gut. Bis heute Abend / Bis dann.
– O.k., bis Samstag.

Saying no and making another suggestion ....

– Das ist mir zu früh/spät. Wie wär's mit …?
– Da muss ich noch arbeiten. Ich kann erst ab …

5.4 Offers

Offering someone something, for example something to eat or drink ....

– Möchten Sie einen Kaffee oder Tee?
– Kann ich Ihnen was zu trinken/essen anbieten?
– Was kann ich Ihnen/dir anbieten?
– Nehmen Sie ein Stück Kuchen?
– Was möchtest du trinken, Weißwein, Rotwein, Bier …?
– Möchtest du ein Eis / ein Bier …?
– Bedienen Sie sich doch.

Accepting an offer ....

– Danke, ja.
– Ja, bitte.
– Ja, sehr gerne.
– Ein Bier, bitte.
– Ich würde gern ein Glas Rotwein trinken.
– Ich hätte am liebsten ein Mineralwasser.

Saying no to an offer ....

– Nein, danke. / Danke, nein.
– Nein, danke, jetzt nicht.
– Für mich bitte nicht.

Explaining why not ....

– Noch etwas Gemüse?	+ Nein, danke, ich bin satt.
– Möchten Sie Nachtisch?	+ Nein, danke, für mich nicht.
– Wie wär's mit einem Cognac?	+ Nein, danke, ich muss noch fahren.

Saying thank you after an invitation ....

– Danke für die Einladung, es war ein wunderbarer Abend.
– Vielen Dank, es war toll. Ich habe mich sehr gut unterhalten.
– Vielen Dank für den netten Abend. Wir müssen leider gehen.
  Der Babysitter kann nur bis 12 Uhr bleiben.

5.5 Making an official appointment

A: Ich hätte gerne einen Termin bei
  Frau Doktor Zorn.
B: Wann geht es bei Ihnen?
A: Montagnachmittags habe ich Zeit.
B: Montag, den 23.4., um 17 Uhr 30.
  Geht das?
A: Geht es etwas früher?
B: 17 Uhr?
A: Ja, das ist gut.

Dr. med. Zorn

Montag, den 23.4.,
um 17 Uhr 30.
Geht das?

Requesting an appointment / Saying when you have time ....

– Ich hätte gerne einen Termin bei Uwe zum Haareschneiden.
– Kann ich am Montag um 13 Uhr kommen?
– Ich kann immer am Nachmittag.

Saying when you do not have time ....

– Am Dienstag kann ich leider nicht.	– Freitag passt mir ganz schlecht.
– Morgens arbeite ich immer.	– Geht es auch etwas früher/später?

6 Conversations

6.1 Beginning a conversation

– Sind Sie geschäftlich hier?
– Kennen Sie Mannheim?
– Ist das Ihr erster Besuch in Österreich?
– Entschuldigung, sind Sie nicht eine Kollegin von Frau Grambitter?
– Ein furchtbares/scheußliches Wetter heute, finden Sie nicht auch?

6.2 Non-committal response / Reaction

– Lassen Sie mich einen Moment überlegen.
– Na ja, eigentlich …

– Was soll ich sagen, …
– Ich weiß nicht, ich denke …

6.3 Showing that you are paying attention and are interested

– Tatsächlich/Wirklich?
– Ich verstehe.

– Hm/Aha.
– Das ist ja interessant.

6.4 Avoiding giving an opinion

– Ich weiß nicht.
– Ich kann/möchte dazu (jetzt / im Moment) nichts sagen.
– Ich bin mir nicht sicher.
– Das ist schwierig zu sagen.

– Es kommt immer darauf an.
– Man kann das so und so sehen.
– Darüber möchte ich (jetzt) nicht sprechen.

6.5 Ending a conversation

– Entschuldigung, aber ich muss jetzt gehen. Rufen Sie mich doch in den nächsten Tagen mal an.
– Es tut mir Leid, aber ich muss dringend telefonieren.
– Sie müssen mich entschuldigen, aber ich habe in zehn Minuten eine Besprechung.
– Ich muss dringend weg. Kann ich Sie/dich später anrufen?
– Entschuldigen Sie mich einen Moment, bitte. Ich möchte nur schnell Dr. Funk begrüßen.

7 Opinions, discussions, likes and dislikes

7.1 Opinions

A: Was hältst du von unserer Umweltministerin?
B: Ich weiß nicht. Ich glaube, sie ist ziemlich kompetent.
A: Meiner Meinung nach ist sie viel zu alt für den Job.

Asking for someone's opinion

– Was hältst du von Peter / dem Direktor / …?
– Wie findest du das Essen im „Sole d'Oro"?
– Was denkst du über …
– Was meinst du zur Steuerreform?

Giving your opinion

– Ich glaube, sie ist in Ordnung.
– Ich halte ihn für sehr intelligent/kompetent/fleißig …
– Meiner Meinung nach ist sie besser geeignet für den Job als er.
– Ich finde, die Pizza schmeckt überhaupt nicht.

Agreeing

– Ja, das glaube ich auch.
– Ich glaube das auch nicht.
– Das stimmt.
– Sie haben Recht. / Du hast Recht.
– Da haben Sie Recht. / Da hast du Recht.

Showing indecision

– Ich weiß nicht.   – Das weiß ich nicht.
– Kann sein.   – Das kann ich nicht beurteilen.
– Vielleicht haben Sie / hast du Recht.

Disagreeing

– Nein, das stimmt nicht.
– Das glaube ich nicht.
– Das ist nicht richtig.
– Ich glaube, das sehen Sie / siehst du falsch.
– Im Gegenteil …

7.2 Expressing certainty, uncertainty

– Ich bin mir sicher, dass …
– Ja, das glaube ich.
– Das nehme ich an.

– Ich bin mir nicht sicher. / Vielleicht.
– Ich weiß nicht.

7.3 Expressing possibility, impossibility

7.4 Saying something is important, unimportant

Saying you think something is important ....

– Das ist sehr wichtig.
– Ich glaube, das ist sehr wichtig.
– Ich halte das für sehr wichtig.

– Das darf man nicht außer Acht lassen.

Saying you think something is unimportant ....

– Das ist nicht so wichtig.
– Ich glaube, das ist nicht so wichtig.

– Ich halte das für unwichtig / nicht so wichtig.

7.5 Likes, dislikes, preferences

Asking if someone likes something/someone	Saying you like something/ someone	Saying you don't like something/someone ....
– Magst du deine neue Chefin?	+ Ich mag meine neue Chefin sehr.	+ Ich finde sie furchtbar.
– Mögen Sie / Magst du türkisches Essen	+ Ja, ich mag türkisches Essen sehr gern.	+ Ich mag türkisches Essen überhaupt nicht.
– Gefällt dir moderne Kunst?	+ Ich finde moderne Kunst sehr interessant.	+ Nein, mir gefallen die Bilder von Rembrandt viel besser.
– Was für Musik magst du?	+ Die neue CD von Gilberto Gil gefällt mir ganz gut.	+ Rockmusik gefällt mir nicht so gut.
		+ Ich finde „Techno" langweilig ...

Asking about preferences, expressing preferences ....

– Mögen Sie / Magst du lieber Wein oder Bier? + Ich trinke lieber Bier.

– Was mögen Sie / magst du lieber, Sommer oder Winter? + Der Sommer ist mir lieber.

– Gefällt Ihnen/dir Mozart oder Bach besser? + Mozart.

– Welches Kleid gefällt Ihnen/dir besser, das rote oder das grüne? + Ich find das grüne viel schöner.

8 Advice, help, warning

8.1 Asking for advice and giving advice

A: Guten Morgen. Ich bin einen Tag in Köln. Was soll ich mir ansehen?
B: Warum gehen Sie nicht zuerst mal in den Dom? Und danach sollten Sie das Wallraf-Richartz-Museum besuchen.

Asking for advice	Giving advice
– Was soll ich tun? Ich habe zehn Kilo zu viel.	+ Ganz einfach: weniger essen! + Du könntest eine Diät machen: wenig Fleisch und Fett, viel Obst und Gemüse. + Ich glaube nicht, dass du eine Diät machen solltest.
– Können Sie mir mir einen Rat geben, wie ich besser Wörter lernen kann?	+ Sie sollten sich eine Lernkartei machen und regelmäßig wieder- holen.
– Ich suche ein gutes Wörterbuch. Haben Sie / Hast du einen Tipp für mich?	+ Kaufen Sie sich / Kauf dir doch ein Lernerwörterbuch.

Accepting/Refusing someone's advice ....

– Gute Idee. – Danke für den Tipp/Rat.	– Na, ich weiß nicht. – Das geht nicht, weil … – Das kann ich nicht machen. …

(→ 📖 B 4)

8.2   Help

Asking for help ....

– Entschuldigung, können Sie mir helfen? …	+ Aber gerne.

Saying you can't help ....

– Leider nein. Mein Bus kommt gerade.
– Tut mir Leid, ich habe keine Zeit.

Offering help ....

– Kann ich dir helfen?
– Soll ich Ihren Koffer tragen?
– Lassen Sie das mich (mal) machen.

Accepting help ....

– Danke, das ist nett von Ihnen/dir.
– Ja, bitte, vielen Dank.

Refusing someone's offer of help ....

– Nein, danke. Es geht schon.
– Vielen Dank. Ich schaffe es schon allein.
– Nein, danke, das ist nicht nötig.

8.3   Sevices/Shopping

A: Können Sie mein Fahrrad reparieren?
B: Sicher, bis wann brauchen Sie es?
A: Geht es bis morgen Nachmittag?
B: Kein Problem.

Asking about services/products ....

– Ich hätte gern zwei Batterien für meinen Walkman.
– Kann ich bei Ihnen diesen Film entwickeln lassen?
– Können Sie mir einen Strauß mit Herbstblumen machen?
– Reparieren Sie auch Schuhe?
– Verkaufen Sie auch Zeitungen/Wörterbücher/Videokassetten …?

8.4   Danger

Warning someone of danger ....

– Vorsicht! Der Topf ist noch heiß.
– Achtung! Da kommt eine Straßen-
  bahn.
– Passen Sie auf, dass Sie nicht aus-
  rutschen. Es ist glatt.
– Seien Sie vorsichtig. Um diese
  Uhrzeit ist der Park gefährlich.
– Nehmen Sie warme Kleidung mit.
  Das Wetter in den Alpen ändert
  sich schnell.
– Feuer!

9 Expressing feelings and moods

Happiness and pleasure ....

– Das freut mich.
– Ich freue mich, das zu hören.

– Ich hab mich sehr darüber gefreut.
– Das ist toll/wunderbar/super/spitze!

Looking forward to something ....

– Ich freue mich auf dich.
– Ich freu mich schon drauf.
– Es wird bestimmt schön/toll/phantastisch ...
– Ich kann es kaum erwarten, dass er kommt.
– Ich freu mich so auf meine Ferien / auf morgen Abend / ...

Surprise ....

– Das ist aber eine Überraschung.
  (more positive)
– Das überrascht mich jetzt aber.
  (negative or positive)
– Das hat mich total überrascht.
  (negative or positive)

– Um Himmels willen! *(negative)*
– Das darf doch nicht wahr sein!
  (negative or positive)
– Sag, dass es nicht wahr ist.
  (usually negative)

Ich hab mir einen Porsche gekauft.

Du? Echt? Das gibt es ja gar nicht!

Annoyance, anger and displeasure ......

– Das ärgert mich wirklich.
– Das ist aber ärgerlich.
– Ich bin echt sauer. *(informal)*
– So ein Mist! *(informal)*

Worry and fear ....

– Ich hab Angst, dass ich die Prüfung nicht bestehe.
– Die Prüfung macht mir wirklich Kummer.
– Mein Sohn macht mir Sorgen.

Relief

– Gott sei Dank! Mein Vater ist wieder gesund.
– Da bin ich aber froh, dass du deine
  Prüfung bestanden hast.
– Ein Glück, dass der ganze Stress vorbei ist.
– Da fällt mir aber ein Stein vom Herzen!

Sadness, grief

– Die letzte Zeit war nicht sehr gut für mich.
– Es geht mir nicht gut in letzter Zeit.
– Ich habe einige persönliche/berufliche Probleme.
– Es ist etwas Schlimmes passiert.
– Ich weiß nicht, wie es weitergehen soll.
– Ich bin immer noch ziemlich traurig.
– Ich komme einfach nicht darüber weg.

Disappointment

– Ich bin sehr enttäuscht.
– Ich bin ziemlich frustriert.
– Das ist aber schade.
– So eine Enttäuschung.
– So hab ich mir das nicht vorgestellt.

Regret, sympathy

– Es tut mir Leid, das zu hören. Wenn ich dir
  helfen kann …
– Das tut mir wirklich Leid.
– Ich kann mir vorstellen, wie du dich fühlst.
– Das ist ja schlimm/furchtbar/entsetzlich …
– Du Armer / Du Arme! *(informal)*

Cheering someone up, optimism

– Machen Sie sich / Mach dir keine Sorgen.
– Das wird schon wieder.
– Lassen Sie sich / Lass dich nicht unterkriegen.
– Ich bin sicher, dass alles wieder gut wird.
– Kopf hoch! *(informal)*

Hope ....

– Hoffentlich klappt alles.
– Wollen wir hoffen, dass alles gut geht.
– Ich hoffe, dass es Ihnen/dir bald wieder gut geht.
– Wir wollen das Beste hoffen.

Doubt, pessimism ....

– Ich bin mir nicht sicher.
– Ich habe meine Zweifel, ob ich das schaffe.
– Ich glaube nicht, dass ich das schaffe.
– Ich kann nicht glauben, dass sich
  etwas ändert.

Indifference, disinterest ....

– Ist doch egal.
– Mir ist es egal.
– Mir ist alles gleich.
– So oder so, mir ist es gleichgültig.
– Was soll's. *(informal)*
– Das ist mir Wurscht. *(informal; south German, A, CH)*

10   Personal information

When dealing with government offices and also when meeting people, you need to be able to give personal information about yourself. In the following examples the expressions you need in government offices are marked with an asterisk *.

10.1   Where you are from / Nationality

Asking where someone is from ....   Saying where you are from ....

– Woher kommen Sie?   + Ich komme aus Polen.
– Woher sind Sie?   + Ich bin aus Polen.
– Aus welchem Land kommen Sie?   + Ich bin Pole/Polin.
– Ihr Heimatland / Ihre Staatsange-
  hörigkeit / Ihre Nationalität, bitte?*

10.2 Place of residence / Address

In German-speaking countries you give the name of the road first and then the number of the house.

Asking where someone lives .... Saying where you live ....

– Wo wohnen Sie / wohnst du?   + Ich wohne in Mannheim.
– Ihr Wohnort, bitte?*   + In Mannheim.
    + Mein Wohnort ist Mannheim.*

– Wie ist Ihre Adresse?   + Meine Adresse/Anschrift ist:
– Ihre Adresse, bitte?*   Merseburger Straße 18
– Wie lautet Ihre Anschrift, bitte?* *(D)*   68231 Mannheim

10.3 Age / date of birth

Asking how old someone is .... Saying how old you are ....

– Wie alt sind Sie?   + Ich bin 30 (Jahre alt).
– Ihr Alter, bitte?*   + 30 Jahre.

Asking when someone was born .... Saying when you were born ....

– Wann sind Sie geboren?*   + Ich bin 1979 geboren.*
– Ihr Geburtsjahr, bitte?*   + 1979.
– An welchem Tag sind Sie geboren?   + Am 17. Mai 1979.
– Wann haben Sie Geburtstag?   + (Ich habe) am 17. Mai (Geburtstag).
– Welches Sternzeichen sind Sie?   + Ich bin Stier.
(→ 📖 B 25)

10.4 Occupation

Asking what someone does .... Saying what you do ....

– Was arbeiten Sie?   + (Ich bin) Mechanikerin.
– Was sind Sie von Beruf?   + Ich arbeite als Mechanikerin.
– Ihr Beruf, bitte?*

10.5 Place of work, employer

Asking where someone works	Saying where you work ....
– Wo arbeiten Sie?	+ (Ich arbeite) in Mannheim.
– In welchem Betrieb arbeiten Sie?	+ Ich arbeite bei der Firma Islinger.
– (Wer ist) Ihr Arbeitgeber, bitte?*	+ Die Firma Islinger.

10.6 Education, training

Saying what kind of education/training you have ....

– Von ... bis ...	habe ich die Grundschule besucht.
– Dann	war ich in der Realschule.
– Anschließend	bin ich auf das Gymnasium gegangen.
– Nachher	habe ich an der Universität ... studiert.
– Danach	habe ich eine Ausbildung als ... gemacht.

– 19..	habe ich meine Ausbildung als ... abgeschlossen.
	habe ich das ICC-Zertifikat gemacht.
	habe ich das Abitur *(D)* / die Matur *(CH)* / die Reifeprüfung *(A)* gemacht.

– Seit 19..	mache ich eine Ausbildung als ...
– Jetzt	besuche ich Weiterbildungskurse an der ...schule.
– Im Moment	mache ich eine Lehre als ...
	studiere ich ... an der Universität.

10.7 Life experience

Giving general information about your past ....

– 19.. habe ich geheiratet.
– Von 19.. bis 19.. habe ich in Ägypten gelebt.
– Drei Jahre lang habe ich in Eisenach gewohnt.
– 19.. habe ich bei Opel gearbeitet.
– Vorher habe ich Informatik studiert.

– Seit 19.. lebe ich in Dresden.

10.8 Family, relatives

.... ♀ .... ⚭ .... ♂ ....

Großmutter	Großeltern	Großvater
Schwiegermutter	Schwiegereltern	Schwiegervater
Mutter	Eltern	Vater
Tante		Onkel
Schwägerin		Schwager
Ehefrau		Ehemann
Schwester		Bruder
Cousine		Cousin
Schwiegertochter		Schwiegersohn
Tochter		Sohn
Nichte		Neffe
Enkelin		Enkel

D + CH: der Cousin, die Cousins; *D* (auch): der Vetter, die Vettern;
D + CH: die Cousine, die Cousinen

▲ Bruder + Schwester (+ ...) = Geschwister

11 Telephone

11.1 Answering the phone, greetings, saying goodbye

In German-speaking countries, when answering your private phone, it is customary to give your surname. Younger people often give their first name as well. It is considered impolite to answer only with the telephone number or to just say Hallo.

When answering a business or office telephone, you usually give the name of the company where you are working first and then your own name.

GHK Lernsysteme, Koenig.
Guten Morgen, was kann ich für Sie tun?

Saying goodbye on the telephone:

– (Auf) Wiederhören. *(formal)*
– Tschüs. *(informal)*

11.2 When the right person doesn't answer

Asking to speak
to someone ....Saying whether or not a person can come to the phone ....

	positive	question	negative
– Kann ich bitte Frau Becker sprechen?	+ Ja, Moment, bitte.	+ Ich werde nachsehen, ob er/sie hier ist.	+ Tut mir Leid, Frau Braun ist heute nicht da.
– Bitte verbinden Sie mich mit Frau Becker.	+ Augenblick, bitte, ich ver- binde Sie.	+ Moment, bitte.	+ Kann ich ihr etwas ausrich- ten?
– Können Sie mich mit Frau Becker verbinden?			
– Ich möchte mit Herrn Becker sprechen, bitte.			

Schäfer.

11.3 Wrong number

⚠ Even when you have the feeling that you have dialed the wrong number, you should give your name and say you are sorry. It is considered extremely impolite to simply hang up.

... Wer ist am Apparat?

– Schäfer.

+ Guten Morgen, hier ist Becker. Entschuldigung, wer ist am Apparat?

– Wetz.

+ Guten Morgen, hier spricht Braun. Ist dort (nicht) Waltz?

Apologizing for a wrong number ....

– Entschuldigen Sie, ich habe falsch gewählt.
– Entschuldigung, ich bin falsch verbunden.
– Tut mir Leid, ich habe die falsche Nummer.
– Pardon *(CH)*, ich habe mich verwählt.

Asking for a telephone number ....

– Ich möchte die Nummer von Herrn Presker in Graz, bitte.
– Ich hätte gern die Nummer von Frau Hanselmann in Berlin.
– Ich brauche die Nummer von … in …
– Geben Sie mir bitte die Nummer von …
– Wie ist die Nummer von …?

When asking for a telephone number from information you have to spell the name. Here is the official German system of words representing the letters of the alphabet which you can learn. Or you can improvise.

Der Name ist Nonner.
N wie „nein",
o wie „oder",
n wie „nein",
n wie „nein", e wie …

A	Anton	N	Nordpol
Ä	Ärger	O	Otto
B	Bertha	Ö	Ökonom
C	Cäsar	P	Paula
Ch	Charlotte	Q	Quelle
D	Dora	R	Richard
E	Emil	S	Samuel
F	Friedrich	T	Theodor
G	Gustav	U	Ulrich
H	Heinrich	Ü	Übermut
I	Ida	V	Viktor
J	Julius	W	Wilhelm
K	Kaufmann	X	Xanthippe
L	Ludwig	Y	Ypsilon
M	Martha	Z	Zacharias

12 Hobbies, interests, relationships

12.1 Leisure activities

Asking about leisure activities .... Saying what your leisure activities are ....

– Was sind Ihre Hobbys?
– Welche Hobbys hast du?
– Was machen Sie in Ihrer Freizeit?
– Wie verbringen Sie Ihre Freizeit?
– Was tust du am liebsten?
– Gehen Sie gerne schwimmen?

+ Ich gehe am liebsten ins Kino.
+ Ich fahre sehr gern Rad.
+ Ich spiele oft Gitarre.
+ Ich spiele sehr gern Tennis.
+ Ich mache am liebsten gar nichts.
+ Nein, ich jogge lieber.
(→ 📖 B 7.5)

12.2 Liking someone, compliments

Saying you like someone ....

Ich finde dich sehr nett.
Du gefällst mir gut/sehr.
Ich mag dich!

Making compliments ....

– Mit dir kann man sich gut unter-
 halten.
– Es macht Spaß, mit dir auszugehen.
– Du siehst gut aus.
(→ 📖 B 7.5, 9)

– Du bist attraktiv.
– Du hast wunderschöne Augen.
– Ich mag dein Lachen so gern.
– Deine Jacke gefällt mir.

13 In a restaurant

13.1 Reserving a table

Reserving a table by telephone ....

– Haben Sie einen Tisch für drei Personen für heute Abend 20 Uhr?
– Ich möchte einen Tisch für drei Personen für heute Abend um 20 Uhr
 reservieren.

When you go to one of the simpler restaurants or cafés in German-speaking countries, it
is completely normal to sit at a table that is already occupied if there are seats free.
Before you sit down, you should ask – Ist hier noch frei? – to ask if it is all right. In
more expensive restaurants it is not nornally acceptable to sit at a table that is already
occupied. It is better to ask the waiter where to sit or the waiter will offer you a table.

13.2 Menus

Asking for a menu ....

– Entschuldigung, können Sie uns die Speisekarte bringen?
– Wir hätten gern die Speisekarte.

Asking what someone likes eating/drinking   Saying what you like eating/drinking ....

positive

– Wie finden Sie Schnitzel?   + Schnitzel mag ich (sehr).
– Mögen Sie Pizza?   + Pizza esse ich (sehr) gern.
– Essen/Trinken Sie gern Tee/Kaffee?   + Tee/Kaffee trinke ich (sehr) gern.
                                             + Das finde ich super.

                                             question
                                             + Was ist das? / Das kenne ich nicht.

                                             negative
                                             + Das mag ich (gar) nicht.
                                             + Das finde ich scheußlich.
                                             + Das esse/trinke ich nicht (gern).

13.3 Choosing something from the menu

Asking what someone would like ....   Suggesting something from the menu ....

– Was isst du?   + Wie wär's mit Pizza?
– Was trinken Sie?   + Nehmen wir Fisch?
– Was nehmen wir?   + Haben Sie Lust auf ...?
– Was bestellst du?
– Was wollen wir nehmen?

Saying what you would like ....

– Ich habe Lust auf einen Salat.
– Ich möchte ein Schnitzel.
– Ich nehme einen Apfelsaft.
– Ich bestelle ...

Hast du Lust auf einen Vorspeisen-teller?

13.4 Ordering and paying the bill

Was darf ich Ihnen bringen?

Für mich bitte ein Steak mit einem gemischten Salat. Und zum Trinken nehme ich einen trockenen Weißwein.

Und ich hätte gern Kalbsschnitzel mit Bratkartoffeln und ein Mineralwasser, bitte.

Asking what someone will have .... Ordering ....

– Ja, bitte?
– Sie wünschen?
– Was hätten Sie gern?
– Was möchten Sie?
– Was wünschen Sie?
– Was darf ich Ihnen bringen?
– Was möchten Sie essen/trinken?

+ Ein Schnitzel, bitte.
+ Wir nehmen zweimal Schnitzel.
+ Ich hätte gern einen Salat.
+ Wir möchten eine Flasche Wein.
+ Bringen Sie mir bitte …
+ Haben Sie Schnitzel?

Asking for something else ....

– Ich hätte gern noch etwas mehr Kartoffeln.
– Könnten Sie mir noch ein Glas Mineralwasser bringen?
– Könnte ich bitte etwas Salz/Pfeffer/… haben?

Paying the bill ....

– Entschuldigung, die Rechnung, bitte.
– Können wir bitte bezahlen?
– Nehmen Sie Kreditkarten/Euroschecks …?

13.5 Sending something back to the kitchen / Complaints

– Entschuldigen Sie, aber das Steak ist durch. Ich wollte medium.
– Das Schnitzel ist kalt / zäh / nicht durch …
– Die Suppe kann ich nicht essen. Sie ist viel zu salzig/fett …

14　In a hotel

14.1　Booking a room

– Ich möchte ein Zimmer für zwei Personen vom 1.3. bis 5.3. reservieren.
– Haben Sie ein Doppelzimmer mit Zusatzbett für eine Nacht?

Kinds of rooms and what they include ....

 Einzelzimmer

 ... mit Bad / Dusche und WC

 Doppelzimmer

 ... mit TV (Fernsehen)

 Dreibettzimmer

 ... mit Telefon

 .. mit Zusatzbett/Kinderbett

Asking about special conditions in the room/hotel ....

– Ist das Zimmer ruhig?
– Liegt das Zimmer zur Straße oder nach hinten raus?
– Ist das Zimmer mit Bad/Dusche/Minibar ...?

– Hat das Zimmer Telefon?
– Gibt es ein Schwimmbad / einen Fitnessraum ...?
– Hat das Hotel einen Parkplatz / eine Garage ...?

Asking about the price ....

– Wie viel kostet ein Doppelzimmer pro Nacht?
– Ist das Frühstück dabei?

– Haben Sie Nichtraucherzimmer?
– Haben Sie Sonderangebote am Wochenende?

14.2　Complaints in a hotel

– Im Bad sind keine Handtücher / ...
– Die Seife / das Toilettenpapier ... fehlt.
– Der Fernseher / die Klimaanlage / das Licht ... funktioniert nicht.
– Im Schrank sind keine / zu wenig Kleiderbügel.
– Das Zimmer ist zu kalt/heiß/laut ...
– Wie kann man die Klimaanlage anmachen/ausmachen?
– Das Zimmer riecht nach Rauch. Ich wollte ein Nichtraucherzimmer.

15　Shopping

15.1　Prices

Asking how much something costs ....　Saying how much something costs ....

– Was macht das?	+ (Das macht) 3 Mark 70.
– Was kostet ein Kilo Tomaten?	+ (Das kostet) 3,70.
– Was kosten 2 Liter Milch?	
– Wie viel kostet dieser Pullover?	
– Wie teuer ist dieser Mantel?	

Currency ....

Schweiz:	1 Schweizer Franken (SFr)	= 100 Rappen
Deutschland:	1 Deutsche Mark (DM)	= 100 Pfennig
Österreich:	1 Österreichischer Schilling (ÖS)	= 100 Groschen
Europa (EWU):	1 Euro	= 100 Cents

15.2　Groceries

Asking what someone would like ....　Asking for something ....

– Ja, bitte?	+ Zwei Bananen, bitte.
– Sie wünschen?	+ Geben Sie mir bitte zwei Bananen.
	+ Ich möchte einen Liter Milch.
	+ Ich hätte gern eine Flasche Cola.
– Noch etwas?	+ Ich brauche noch ein Kilo ...
– Ist das alles?	+ Haben Sie Bananen?

15.3　Books, records, videos, etc

– Ich suche das Buch „Grieche sucht Griechin" von Dürrenmatt.
– Ich hätte gern den CD-ROM Reiseführer über Polen.
– Haben Sie das Video „Der König der Löwen"?
– Gibt es diesen Roman auch als Film?

Often you will be	– Können Sie mir den Verlag angeben?
asked to give more	– Wissen Sie, wer der Autor ist?
details:	– Wissen Sie, wo/wann das erschienen ist?

15.4 Cloth shops

Asking for an article of clothing ....

– Ich suche einen Pulli mit langen
  Ärmeln.
– Ich möchte ein Kleid in Größe 44.
– Ich hätte gern eine Jacke in Blau.
– ... aus Seide/Wolle ...

– Haben Sie den/diesen Pulli in
  meiner Größe?
– Hätten Sie das/dieses Kleid in
  Größe 44?
– Gibt es die/diese Jacke eine
  Nummer größer/kleiner?

Saying that an article of clothing
fits or looks good on someone ....   Reaction ....

– Das steht Ihnen prima.
– Das sitzt sehr gut.
– Das entspricht genau Ihrem Typ.

+ Aber die Farbe gefällt mir nicht.
+ Es ist mir etwas zu eng/weit/kurz ...
+ Es gefällt mir (nicht).

16 Changing money

Asking for change ....

– Können Sie (mir) das wechseln?
– Ich brauche etwas Kleingeld für den Automaten.
– Haben Sie vielleicht fünf Zehner/Zehn-Pfennig-Stücke für mich?
– Entschuldigung, ich brauche zwei Markstücke für die Parkuhr.

Exchanging currency ....

– Ich möchte 100 Dollar in DM wechseln.
– Ich hätte gern für 100 Franken argentinische Pesos.
– Geben Sie mir bitte 100 US-Dollar.

When you want to exchange currency, you
usually go to a bank or currency exchange
bureau (eg at the train station).

▲ If you have an Eurocheque card or one
of the more prominent credit cards you can
also withdraw money directly from banking
machines at most banks. Limits and fees
are usually posted.

17 At the post office

Sending a letter/parcel ....

– Mit Luftpost, bitte.
– Als Einschreiben, bitte.
– Als Eilbrief/Eilpaket, bitte.

Asking for specific information ....

– Was kostet ein Paket nach Ägypten?
– Wie schwer darf ein Luftpostpaket nach Singapur sein?
– Wie lange braucht ein Paket per Schiff nach Japan?

Having mail forwarded or held ....

– Ich fahre weg. Können Sie meine Post lagern?
– Können Sie mir die Post nachsenden?

The post office in Germany has recently been privatized and its previous monopoly
has been abolished in most instances. Because of this, there are more and more
other companies that offer postal services for parcels and letters in addition to the
"Deutsche Post AG".

18 At the train station

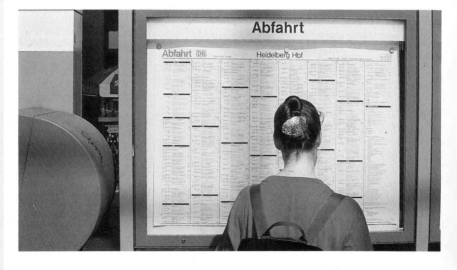

– Entschuldigung, wann fährt der nächste Zug nach Chemnitz?
– Um wie viel Uhr gibt es einen Zug nach Frankfurt?

– Wie lange braucht der Zug bis Leipzig?
– Gibt es einen schnelleren Zug?
– Brauche ich einen IC-Zuschlag?
– Gibt es Sonderangebote?
– Gibt es Ermäßigungen für Kinder/Studenten/Rentner/Familien …
– Lohnt es sich, eine BahnCard zu kaufen? *(D)*

– Entschuldigung, wo finde ich den Auskunftsschalter?
– Auf welchem Gleis fährt der Zug nach Dresden?
– Hält dieser Zug in Prenzlau?
– Wo muss ich umsteigen?

– Ist das ein ICE (Intercityexpress-zug)?
– Hat dieser Zug einen Speisewagen?
– Wo sind die Wagen der zweiten Klasse?

Buying a train ticket ....

– Einmal nach Mainz, einfach, zweite Klasse, bitte.
– Eine Rückfahrkarte *(D)* nach Frankfurt an der Oder, bitte.
– Einmal Salzburg hin und zurück, bitte.
– Ein Billett *(CH)* nach Chur, retour *(CH)*, erste Klasse, bitte.

⚠ At many train stations, as well as in streetcars and buses, you can (and sometimes have to) buy your ticket from a machine.

19 Illness, physical complaints

19.1 Asking about someone's health

A: Was ist denn mit dir los? Bist du krank?
B: Ich weiß nicht. Ich glaube, ich habe die Grippe.
A: Oh je. Hast du etwas zum Einnehmen?
B: Nein, aber ich gehe gleich zum Arzt.

Asking how someone is	Reaction ....
– Sie sehen / Du siehst aber nicht sehr gut aus. Bist du krank?	+ Nein, es ist alles in Ordnung. + Ja, ich habe etwas Kopfweh/ Bauchweh …
– Fühlen Sie sich / Fühlst du dich (nicht) gut?	+ Mir geht es nicht gut. Ich glaube, ich habe …
– Haben Sie / Hast du noch Fieber/ Halsweh … ?	+ Es geht mir besser, danke. + Ich habe noch Fieber/Halsweh …
– Was hat der Arzt gesagt?	
– Wann dürfen Sie / darfst du wieder arbeiten/aufstehen … ?	+ Übermorgen (kann ich wieder arbeiten/aufstehen …).

19.2 Expressing your regret/sympathy

negative	*positive*
– Das tut mir Leid.	– Das ist gut.
– Das ist ja schlimm.	
– Oh je.	

19.3 At the doctor's

Doctor	Patient
– Was fehlt Ihnen?	+ Ich habe …
– Wo tut es weh?	+ Im Hals / Hier an der Hand …
– Wo haben Sie Schmerzen?	+ Im rechten Ohr …
– Was führt Sie zu mir?	+ Ich fühle mich …
– Wie lange haben Sie das schon?	+ Seit …
– Haben Sie das schon einmal gehabt?	+ Nein, das ist das erste Mal.

Saying you are ill / where it hurts ....

– Ich habe Bauchweh/Halsweh/Zahnweh …
– Ich habe Bauchschmerzen/Magenschmerzen/Halsschmerzen/ Zahnschmerzen …
– Ich habe Fieber/Schnupfen/(die) Grippe/Durchfall …
– Ich habe mich erbrochen.
– Ich bin krank/erkältet …
– Ich fühle mich nicht gut / nicht wohl / schlecht / fiebrig …

What the doctor prescribes ....

– Ich schreibe Ihnen ein Rezept für …
– Holen Sie sich das in der Apotheke.
– Nehmen Sie das dreimal täglich.
– Kommen Sie am Freitag wieder.
  Meine Sprechstundenhilfe gibt
  Ihnen einen Termin.

20   Directions / How to get from here to there

To give someone directions or tell someone the way, you need prepositions
(→ 📖 C 77–82) and adverbs (→ 📖 C 90–91).

20.1   Directions

aufwärts   abwärts   vorwärts   rückwärts
nach oben   nach unten   nach vorn   nach hinten
rauf   runter   vor   zurück

20.2   How to get there

Asking the way ....

– Entschuldigung, bitte.   – Wie finde ich den Bahnhof?
– Können Sie mir helfen?   – Wo ist (hier) der Bahnhof?
                                      – Ich suche das Rathaus.
                                      – Wie komme ich zur U-Bahn-Halte-
                                        stelle?
                                      – Wo geht es hier zum Paradeplatz?
                                      – Ich möchte zur Hegelstraße.

wieder - again   durch - thought

Describing the way ....

Wir fahren zum Bauern

– Gehen Sie / Fahren Sie …

gehen Sie
… 200 Meter
geradeaus.

First
… die erste
Straße rechts.

… nach links.

… über die
Straße.

… über die
Brücke.

… über den Platz.
der Platz

… hinter das
Haus.

… vor das Haus.

… die Straße
entlang.
along

… um die Ecke.
around the corner

through
… durch den
Wald.

… nach Ober-
hausen.

… (bis) zum
Bahnhof.

… an der Kirche
vorbei.

… aus der Stadt
(heraus*).

… ins Dorf
(hinein*).

*In everyday German,
people often use
the words: raus,
rein, rauf, runter.

… um die Kirche
(herum*).

… die Treppe
hinauf*.

… die Treppe
hinunter*.

20.3 Public transport: buses, streetcars, subways, etc

A: Entschuldigung, wie komme ich nach Feudenheim?
B: Nehmen Sie die Straßenbahnlinie 32.

A: Können Sie mir sagen, welcher Bus ins Zentrum fährt?
B: Die (Nummer) 79.

– Fahren Sie bis zum Hauptbahnhof.
– Steigen Sie am Hauptbahnhof in die Linie 41 um.
– Fahren Sie zwei Stationen weiter, dann sind Sie am Wasserturm.

20.4 Names of places (countries, cities, etc)

With names of places, you use the preposition nach to answer the question Wohin?

⚠ Some place names, as well as names of geographical regions, are always used with an article. In these cases you usually use the preposition in:

– Wir reisen nach Deutschland.
– Ich fahre nach Villach.

– Ich fahre …

… in den Irak.
… in den Iran.
… in den Libanon.
… in den Sudan.

… ins Kleine Walsertal.
… ins Schlitzer Land.
… ins Rothaargebirge.

… in die Schweiz.
… in die Türkei.

… in die Niederlande.
… in die USA.

⚠ But:
– Ich fahre an den Bodensee.
– Ich fahre ans Mittelmeer.

21 Place and location

To describe where someone or something is located in relationship to someone or something else you use prepositions (→ 📖 C 77–82) and adverbs (→ 📖 C 90–91).

21.1 Describing where someone or something is

This is how you can say where someone or something is ....

21.2 Describing where a place is located

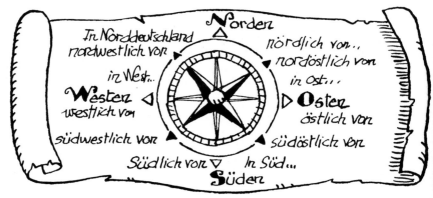

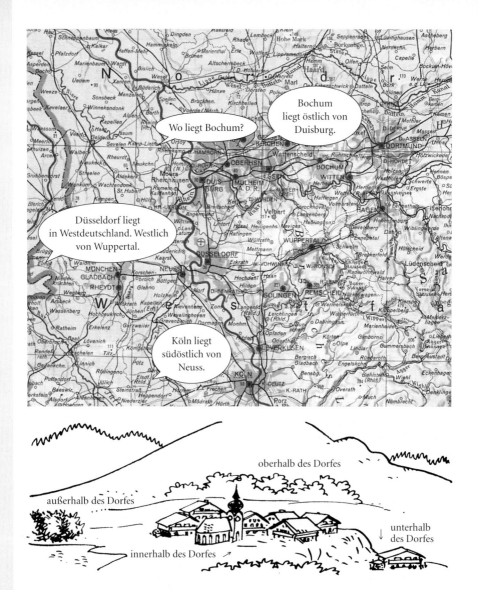

Saying where a building is ....

– Das Rathaus ist in der Poststraße.
– Das Museum liegt am Fluss.
– Die Kirche befindet sich gegenüber dem Rathaus / … außerhalb der Stadt / hinter dem Schloss.

22.1 Opening and closing forms for personal letters

– Hallo, Paul / Hallo, Irmgard
– Lieber Paul / Liebe Irmgard
– Liebe Familie Meier
– Lieber Herr Hug / Liebe Frau Weißling

– Alles Liebe	– Viele herzliche Grüße
– Viele Grüße	– Mit herzlichen Grüßen
– Liebe Grüße	– Herzlich grüßt Wolfgang
– Herzliche Grüße von	

Mario Irmisch
R. Marchal Machado, 520
001-06228 São Paulo
Brasilien

Nina Irmisch
Poststraße 27
68535 Edingen-Neckarhausen
Alemanha

São Paulo, 28.2.1999

Liebe Nina,

jetzt bin ich schon seit zwei Wochen von zu Hause weg und muss noch drei Wochen bleiben. Die Arbeit ist interessant, aber es fällt mir schon schwer.

Ich vermisse dich sehr und denke jeden Tag an dich! Lass es dir gut gehen und grüße alle von mir.

Alles Liebe,

dein Mario

22.2 Business letters

Openings and endings ....

– Sehr geehrter Herr Hug,	– Mit freundlichen Grüßen
– Sehr geehrte Frau Dr. Müller,	– Mit freundlichem Gruß
– Sehr geehrte Herren,	– Freundliche Grüße
– Sehr geehrte Damen,	
– Sehr geehrte Damen und Herren,	

Form ....

Here is one form for letters that is often used.
There are, however, many variations.

Place and date
↓

Sender → Sandra Zawadska
               Otto-Beck-Straße 10
               68129 Mannheim
               Tel. 0621 9 85 38
                                                      Mannheim, 2.9.1998

Addressee → Frau E. Spiess
               Berliner Straße 396
               69188 Heidelberg

Heading → 3-Zimmer-Wohnung in Leimen

Opening → Sehr geehrte Frau Spiess,

Body → in der Rhein-Neckar-Zeitung vom 1.9.1998 habe ich gelesen, dass Sie zum
1. Oktober 1998 eine 3-Zimmer-Wohnung in Leimen vermieten.

Ich interessiere mich sehr für diese Wohnung. Ich bin Polin, 25 Jahre alt, ledig,
Nichtraucherin. Mein Arbeitgeber ist die Firma BAP in Walldorf.

Ich würde mich freuen, bald von Ihnen zu hören.

Ending → Mit freundlichen Grüßen

Signature → *Sandra Zawadska*

When you are applying for a position, it is most important to include information about your life.

A written application should include a letter of application (→ 📖 B 23.1), a CV (→ 📖 B 23.2), copies of any school diplomas or degrees and, if possible, referrees (addresses of people from whom the company can request further information about the applicant).

Uns fehlt der/die
berufserfahrene, dynamische, zuverlässige

Kaufmännische Angestellte

mit Eigeninitiative und Fähigkeit zur Teamarbeit. PC-Kenntnisse notwendig.
Herrn Werner Herold, REMM (Recycling Maschinen Mauer AG), Industriestraße 3, 69256 Mauer

23.1 Letter of application

The rules which apply to a business letter also apply to a letter of application:

Lisa Danzer
Martinsgasse 7
69151 Neckargemünd
Tel/Fax: 06223-5 67 23
E-Mail: LDanzer@t-online.de   ← Sender

Neckargemünd, 9. Mai 1999

Place ↑   ↑ Date

REMM   ← Addressee
Herrn Werner Herold
Industriestraße 3
69256 Mauer

Stellenangebot in der RNZ vom 8.5.1999   ← Reason for writing

Sehr geehrter Herr Herold,   ← Opening

in Ihrer Anzeige in der RNZ vom 8. Mai suchen Sie eine kaufmännische Angestellte. Ich möchte mich um diese Stelle bewerben.

Seit 1991 bin ich als kaufmännische Angestellte bei der DIRECT-Bank in Frankfurt tätig. Vor einem Monat sind wir aber nach Neckargemünd gezogen, weil mein Mann eine Stelle bei der Heidelberger Druckmaschinen AG angenommen hat. Deshalb suche ich jetzt eine Stelle im Raum Heidelberg.

In unserem Betrieb arbeiten wir seit vielen Jahren mit Computern und Netzwerken. Vor zwei Wochen habe ich außerdem einen Lehrgang der Bürowirtschaft abgeschlossen. Aus den Anlagen können Sie weitere Details zu meiner Ausbildung und meiner Berufstätigkeit entnehmen.

Ich denke, dass meine bisherigen Berufserfahrungen in Ihrem Betrieb von Nutzen sein können, und würde mich über eine Antwort und einen Termin für ein persönliches Gespräch freuen. Tagsüber bin ich unter der oben genannten Telefonummer zu erreichen.

Mit freundlichen Grüßen   ← Ending

Lisa Danzer

Anlagen: ← Enclosures
Lebenslauf mit Bild
zwei Zeugniskopien

Application
Employment situation (occupation/company/place)
Work experience
Mention enclosures
Appointment for an interview
Telephone number

Buildings blocks for a letter of application ....

[Return address]   [Place, date]

[Addressee]

Stellenangebot in … vom …

– Sehr geehrte Frau …
– Sehr geehrter Herr …
– Sehr geehrte Damen und Herren

– In Ihrer Anzeige in … vom … suchen Sie eine/n …
– Ich beziehe mich auf Ihre Anzeige in … vom…, in der Sie eine/n … suchen.

– Ich bewerbe mich um diese Stelle.
– Mit diesem Schreiben bewerbe ich mich um die ausgeschriebene Stelle.

– Zur Zeit arbeite ich als … bei (der) … in …
– Im Moment bin ich als … bei der Hypo-Bank in … tätig.
– Bis vor drei Monaten habe ich als … bei der … gearbeitet. Leider wurde der Betrieb geschlossen. Seitdem bin ich arbeitslos.

– Ich möchte mich beruflich verändern, weil …
– Ich suche eine neue Stelle, da …

– … ich vor kurzem nach … gezogen bin.
– … ich am jetzigen Arbeitsplatz keine Aufstiegsmöglichkeiten habe.

– Details über meinen beruflichen Werdegang können Sie den Anlagen entnehmen.
– Weitere Informationen über meine Person finden Sie in der Anlage.

– Ich würde mich freuen, wenn Sie meine Bewerbung berücksichtigen würden, und bitte um einen Gesprächstermin.
– Über eine positive Antwort und einen Termin für ein Gespräch würde ich mich sehr freuen.

– Sie erreichen mich telefonisch unter der Nummer …

Mit freundlichen Grüßen

Anlagen: tabellarischer Lebenslauf mit Lichtbild, Zeugniskopien, Referenzen

23.2 CV

You should also include a CV in tabular form with an application. There are many different possibilities. Here is an example.

TABELLARISCHER LEBENSLAUF

1. Persönliches

Familienname	Danzer
Vorname	Lisa
Geburtstag	21.3.1966
Geburtsort	Neckarhausen
Eltern	Johann Danzer, Verwaltungsangestellter
	Elsbeth Danzer, Verkäuferin

2. Schulausbildung

1972–1976	Grundschule in Neckarhausen
1976–1982	Joh.-Kepler-Realschule in Heidelberg

3. Berufsausbildung

1982–1985	Ausbildung zur kaufmännischen Angestellten bei der Boehringer GmbH in Mannheim

4. Berufstätigkeit

1986–Mai 1990	Kaufmännische Angestellte im Rechnungswesen bei Boehringer
Juni 1990–Mai 1998	DIRECT-Bank Frankfurt

5. Besondere Kenntnisse und Fertigkeiten

Sprachen	Englisch
Computer	PC (Microsoft Word, Excel, Netzwerkkenntnisse)

Neckargemünd, 9.5.1999

Lisa Danzer

24 Demands, orders, don'ts

24.1 Demands and orders (Please → 📖 B 4)

There are different ways of formulating demands and orders:

using the imperative form of a verb (→ 📖 C 20.5)

– Öffnen Sie (doch) das Fenster!
– Mach (sofort) die Tür zu!

using the modal verbs müssen and sollen (→ 📖 C 27.2)

– Sie müssen unbedingt das Fenster öffnen, man kommt ja um vor Hitze!
– Du sollst die Tür zumachen, hab ich gesagt!

using the infinitive form of a verb (→ 📖 C 22)

– Das Fenster öffnen!
– Die Tür zumachen!

⚠ The difference between requesting, demanding and ordering often depends on the intonation and the use of the word bitte.

24.2 Don'ts, warnings

There are various ways of formulating don'ts and warnings:

using the imperative form of a verb + negation (→ 📖 C 20.5)

announcement in an aeroplane:
– Bringen Sie die Rückenlehnen Ihrer Sitze in aufrechte Position.
  Rauchen Sie nicht! …
father to child:
– Fass das nicht an. Es ist heiß!

using the modal verbs dürfen and sollen + negation (→ 📖 C 27.2)

– Sie dürfen nicht rauchen!
– Du sollst keinen Alkohol trinken!

using the infinitive of a verb + negation (→ 📖 C 22)

– Bitte die Kunstwerke nicht berühren.
– Elektronische Geräte nicht während des Fluges benutzen.

25 Time days and dates

25.1 Time of day

The official way of telling the time (that you hear at stations, airports, on the radio, on TV, etc.) is relatively easy to understand.

10.11 Uhr zehn Uhr elf
10.40 Uhr zehn Uhr vierzig
10.45 Uhr zehn Uhr fünfundvierzig

In everyday life the way of telling the time is much more complicated.

10.00 Uhr   (Punkt) zehn   – Es ist genau zehn.
10.05 Uhr   fünf nach zehn   – Es ist kurz nach zehn.
10.10 Uhr   zehn nach zehn
10.15 Uhr   Viertel nach zehn / viertel elf*
10.20 Uhr   zwanzig nach zehn
10.25 Uhr   fünf vor halb elf   – Es ist gleich halb elf.
10.30 Uhr   halb elf
10.35 Uhr   fünf nach halb elf
10.40 Uhr   zwanzig vor elf
10.45 Uhr   Viertel vor elf / drei viertel elf*
10.50 Uhr   zehn vor elf
10.55 Uhr   fünf vor elf   – Es ist gleich / kurz vor elf.
11.00 Uhr   (Punkt) elf

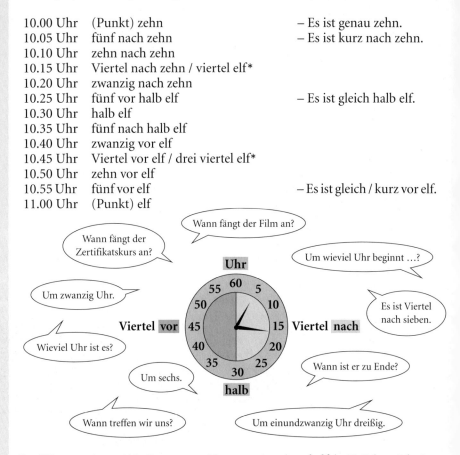

*In different regions within German-speaking countries viertel elf (=10.15) and drei-viertel elf (=10.45) are much more common than in others. You don't necessarily have to be able to use these forms actively, but it is very helpful to be able to under stand them when you hear them.

Asking the time of day	Saying what time it is ....
– Wie viel Uhr ist es bitte? – Wie spät ist es bitte?	+ Es ist 6 (Uhr) / genau 6 … + 6 Uhr 15 / Viertel nach 6.
– Wann beginnt das Fest? – Um wie viel Uhr kommst du?	+ Um halb 7 / 18 Uhr 30.

25.2 Days of the week, months of the year, years and seasons

Day	Abbreviation	Month	Abbreviation
Montag	Mo	Januar	Jan.
Dienstag	Di	Februar	Febr.
Mittwoch	Mi	März	–
Donnerstag	Do	April	Apr.
Freitag	Fr	Mai	–
Samstag/Sonnabend	Sa	Juni	–
Sonntag	So	Juli	–
		August	Aug.
		September	Sept.
		Oktober	Okt.
		November	Nov.
		Dezember	Dez.

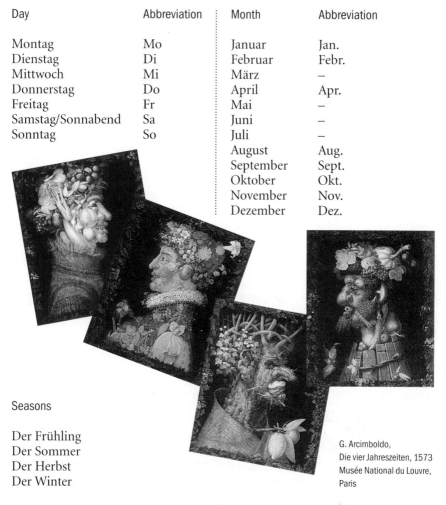

G. Arcimboldo,
Die vier Jahreszeiten, 1573
Musée National du Louvre,
Paris

Seasons

Der Frühling
Der Sommer
Der Herbst
Der Winter

Asking for the day of the week	Giving the day of the week ....
– Welcher Wochentag ist heute?	+ Mittwoch.
– Welchen Wochentag haben wir heute?	+ Heute ist Mittwoch.
– Wann ist das Konzert?	+ Am Samstag.
– An welchem Tag treffen wir uns?	+ Am nächsten Sonntag.

25.3 Dates

There are two possibilities you can use to give the date:

Ordinal number + month: der siebzehnte Mai

Ordinal number + ordinal number: der siebzehnte Fünfte

Date	– Heute ist …	– Ich komme …
01.01.	der erste Januar.	am ersten Januar.
02.02.	der zweite Februar.	am zweiten Februar.
03.03.	der dritte März.	am dritten März.
04.04.	der vierte April.	am vierten April.
05.05.	der fünfte Mai.	am fünften Mai.
06.06.	der sechste Juni.	am sechsten Juni.
07.07.	der siebte Juli.	am siebten Juli.
08.08.	der achte August.	am achten August.
09.09.	der neunte September.	am neunten September.
10.10.	der zehnte Oktober.	am zehnten Oktober.
11.11.	der elfte November.	am elften November.
12.12.	der zwölfte Dezember.	am zwölften Dezember.

(Ordinal numbers → 📖 C 76, Anhang 1.1)

Asking what the date is	Saying what the date is ....
– Der Wievielte / Welcher Tag ist heute bitte?	+ Der 17. Mai.
	+ Heute ist der 17. Mai.
– Wann hast du Geburtstag?	+ Am 17. Mai.
– Am Wievielten / An welchem Tag ist das Konzert?	+ Am 17.5.

Wann haben wir die Sitzungen mit der REMM AG?

Die sind am dreizehnten Mai um neun und am fünfzehnten um 16 Uhr.

26 Weather

Talking about the weather ....

This is how it looks:	This is in the newspaper:	This is how you talk about it:
	– Es ist sonnig. – Die Sonne scheint. – Es ist schönes Wetter.	– Ein Super-Wetter haben wir heute! – Schönes Wetter heute, nicht? – Ein richtiges Bilderbuchwetter!
	– Es ist leicht bewölkt. – leichte Bewölkung – Aufhellungen	– Hm, nicht mehr so schön wie gestern.
	– Es ist stark bewölkt. – Es ist bedeckt. – Bewölkungszunahme	– Heute gibt es sicher noch Regen. – Ziemlich grau heute!

– Es regnet.
– Es ist regnerisch.
– Niederschläge
– starke Regenfälle

– Schlechtes Wetter heute!
– So ein Sauwetter!
– Mistwetter!

– Es gibt ein Gewitter.
– Es blitzt und donnert.
– Gewitterneigung
– Unwetter

– Was für ein schreckliches
  Gewitter!

– Es schneit.
– Schneefälle
– Wintereinbruch

– Ist das eine Kälte!
– Brr, ist das kalt!

– Es ist neblig.
– Nebel

– So ein Nebel!
– Man sieht ja kaum die Hand vor
  den Augen!

– starker Westwind
– Winde aus West(en)
– Es ist stürmisch.

– Ziemlich windig heute.
– Ein Wind ist das heute!

– Es ist sehr warm.
– Es ist heiß.
– hohe Temperaturen

– Puh, ist das heiß!
– Eine Affenhitze haben wir heute!

From:
Dr. Heinrich
Hoffmann,
Der fliegende Robert

Speaking and writing

1 Sounds and letters

The basic building blocks of every language are its sounds. When we speak, we produce a series of different sounds that mean something when we put them together. When someone listening to us understands what we have said, it means that they were able to decode these sounds. Many different systems have been devised in order to put languages "onto paper". One of these is the Latin alphabet. The German variant of this alphabet contains 26 letters and three additional symbols with so-called umlauts (two dots placed over a vowel: ä, ö, ü).

איך האב דיך ליב

私は貴方が好きてナ

I love you!

ΣΕΑΓΑΠΩ

我 愛 你

Ich liebe dich!

A Ä B C D E F G H I J K L M N O Ö P Q R S T U Ü V W X Y Z

a ä b c d e f g h i j k l m n o ö p q r s t u ü v w x y z

The letters represent the various sounds in a written form, but there is no one-to-one correspondence between the letters and the sounds. The same letter or group of letters can represent more than one sound and one sound can be represented by different letters or groups of letters. Here are two examples:

Vogel   Fahrrad

The V and the F represent the same sound here.

Vogel   Vase

Here, the V in Vase sounds about the same as the English V, or the German W in Würfel.

In spite of such irregularities, it is still much easier to figure out from its spelling how a German word is pronounced, than it is for an English word.

The pronunciation of German differs considerably from region to region. There is still, however, a "standard" in each of the three German-speaking countries. News reports on TV, for example, will usually be read in this "standard language".

2   Sounds, word stress and sentence stress

We can separate sounds into three different categories:

Vowels	a, ä, e, i, o, ö, u, ü	Mann, Mädchen, Kind, Foto, Kurs
Diphthongs	au, ei, eu	Frau, Einheit, Deutsch
Consonants	b, c, h, sch ...	begrüßen, Hotel, Schule

Some vowels are long (Mädchen) and some are short (Mann).

The best way to learn pronunciation is by practising a lot: both listening and speaking. Listening actively is as important as speaking. Without listening to the different sounds in a language, you cannot learn to produce them yourself.

Depending on which sounds you already use in your mother tongue, certain German sounds will be easier or more difficult for you to pick out and then produce yourself. For this reason, rather than listing a lot of complicated rules for pronunciation, **euro-lingua** will instead concentrate on two aspects of intonation: where the stress comes in words and where it comes in sentences.

2.1   Word stress

Words are made up of syllables. Some words have one syllable (Frau) and others have two (Ho-tel) or more. When a word has more than one syllable, the syllables are stressed differently. One of the syllables has the word stress.

In the vocabulary list in the course book and in the vocabulary booklet, we have marked the stressed vowel as follows: long _ and short .

In different dictionaries you will find different symbols. In the international phonetic alphabet, which a lot of dictionaries use, the word stress is shown as follows:

Mädchen   ['mɛːtçən]
Hotel   [hoˈtɛl]

The stress mark comes before the syllable that is stressed.

In German, there are a lot of words that come from other languages. In most (native) German words, the stress comes on the first syllable:

Kurs, Kurs-lei-te-rin, le-sen, A-bend, Na-me, hei-ßen

In foreign words, it often comes somewhere else:

Com-pu-ter, Po-li-tik, Kon-fe-renz, Tou-rist

2.2 Sounds

In the following table we have listed the most important sounds in standard, or high, German and the various ways in which they are written. (Many native speakers will produce these sounds using slight variations. Don't worry about it too much and eventually you will start having fun "figuring out" accents.)

1 Vowels

Vowel	Spelling	Examples
<a> (long)	a	haben, Tag, Lage
	aa	waagerecht
	ah	Bahnhof
<a> (short)	a	Samstag, hat, Stamm
<e> (long)	e	er, werden
	ee	Idee
	eh	gehen
<e> (short)	e (rare)	Telefon, Rezeption
<i> (long)	i	wir
	ie	lieben
	ih	ihr
	ieh	ziehen
<i> (short)	i	Gitarre, richtig, mit
<o> (long)	o	Monat, so, hoch
	oo	Zoo
	oh	ohne
<o> (short)	o	modern, oft, Sonntag, Osten
<u> (long)	u	gut, Schule, du, Buch
	uh	Kuh
<u> (short)	u	Musik, Kurs, Wunsch

Vowel	Spelling	Examples
<ä> (long)	ä	Mädchen, Sekretärin
	äh	Nähe
<ä> (short)	ä	Plätze
	e (very common)	lernen, Herr, erkennen
<ö> (long)	ö	hören, Brötchen
	öh	Söhne
<ö> (short)	ö	Wörter, möchte
<ü> (long)	ü	Übung, Schüler
	üh	Stühle
	y	Typ
<ü> (short)	ü	Büro, müssen

2 Diphthongs (two vowels or vowel sounds together)

Diphthong	Spelling	Examples
<au>	au	aus, rauchen
<ai>	ei	ein, heißen
	eih	Reihenfolge
	ey (very rare)	Meyer
	ai	Mai
	ay (very rare)	Mayer
<oü>	äu	äußern, Häuser
	eu	Eule, Freund
	oi (very rare)	Konvoi, Ahoi!

3 Consonants

Consonant .... Most common spelling .... Examples ....

Consonant	Most common spelling	Examples
<b>	b	Bild, leben
	bb	knabbern
<d>	d	deutsch, wieder
	dd	addieren
<g>	g	gehen, glauben, morgen
	gg	Flagge
<p>	p	Post, April
	pp	Gruppe
	b	ab, gelb
<t>	t	Tochter, eigentlich
	tt	Wetter
	th	Theater
	d	Geld
	dt	Stadt
<k>	k	Kurs, Mechaniker
	ck	backen
	g	Tag
	c	Computer, Cafeteria
	ch	Chur, Charakter
<h>	h	heute, Krankenhaus, Aha!
<j>	j	jetzt, ja
<f>	f	fahren, Anfang
	ff	Giraffe
	v	Vogel, viel, aktiv
	ph	Alphabet, Biographie

Consonant	Most common spelling	Example
<w>	w	was, Wort
	ww (rare)	Struwwelpeter
	wh (rare)	Whisky
	v	Verb, Vokabular, Vase
<l>	l	Land, Maler
	ll	Tabelle
<m>	m	machen, Nomen
	mm	kommen
<n>	n	nicht, Information
	nn	Freundinnen
<r>	r	richtig
	rr	Terrasse
	rh (rare)	Rhein
<s>	s	sagen, Musik, das, was
	ss	Adresse
	ß	heißen, Fuß, groß
	z	Quiz, Bronze
<z>	z	Zahl, Notiz
	zz	Skizze
	tz	Katze
	ts	Rätsel
	c (rare)	Cäsar
<x>	x	Taxi, Text
<ch>	ch	ach, hoch, Buch; sich, euch, Milch, Chemie
<sch>	sch	Schuhe, Flasche, falsch
<ng>	ng	bringen, Zeitung

2.3 Sentence stress

By changing the stress in a sentence, we can change its meaning quite radically.

1. Das ist mein <u>Freund</u>. (not my brother or husband or lover)
2. <u>Das</u> ist mein Freund. (not the other man standing there)
3. Das ist <u>mein</u> Freund! (not yours or hers or his)

Intonation, in other words the way in which the voice rises or falls when speaking, depends on a lot of different factors.

– Intonation shows the speaker's attitude to the content of what he or she is saying. It is possible to say the same sentence in a friendly or angry way without changing the grammar at all.

– Intonation differs according to region. For example the "melody" of the language in Hamburg is very different to that in Vienna and the one in Bern different to the one in Dresden.

– Intonation also depends on the situation in which the speaker is speaking: whether it is at the office, between friends, in court, etc.

Words and sentences

3 Introduction

Every language consists of words.

Abend Name mein Müller ist guten

When the words are put together according to special rules, sentences and texts are formed.

Guten Abend, mein Name ist Müller.

Grammar describes how words in a language can be altered and put together to form sentences and texts.

4 Word types (parts of speech)

There are different types of words (or parts of speech). In most sentences there is more than one type of word. Here we provide you with a short summary of the most important types, so that you can become familiar with their grammatical terms. There is more information about each word type in the appropriate part of this grammar section.

Word type	Examples	Example in a sentence
Verbs	heißen, lesen	Ich **heiße** Hassan Askari.
Nouns	Kurs, Teilnehmer	Der **Kurs** hat 15 **Teilnehmer.**
Articles	der, das, die, ein, eine	**Das** Kursbuch hat 256 Seiten.
Pronouns	ich, Ihnen, manche	**Ich** lesen **Ihnen** die Liste vor.
Determiners	mein, diese, viele	**Mein** Name ist Müller.
Adjectives	interessant, groß, schön	Ich lese ein **interessantes** Buch.
Prepositions	in, auf, bei	Ich wohne **in** Seckenheim.
Conjunctions	und, aber, weil	Ich wohne in Seckenheim **und** arbeite in Mannheim.
Adverbs	heute, zuerst, hier	**Heute** arbeite ich nicht.

5 Conjugation, declension, comparison

In German, a lot of words can change their form. A verb takes on different forms, depending on person and tense (conjugation). Nouns, pronouns, determiners and adjectives take different endings, depending on case (declension). Adjectives have different comparative forms. Many word types have both singular and plural forms.

Here are a few examples to acquaint you with the terms. You can find more information in the following chapters of the grammar section.

Word type	Various forms		Examples
Verbs	*Person*		Ich arbeite bis 13 Uhr und du arbeitest dann bis 18 Uhr. Danach arbeitet dann Peter bis 22 Uhr.
	Tense	*Present*	Ich arbeite jeden Tag.
		Simple past	Bis 1997 arbeitete er bei VW.
		Perfect etc	Ich **habe** bis 1997 bei VW **gearbeitet.**
	Mood	*Indicative*	Ich arbeite.
		Subjunctive	Ich **würde** ja arbeiten, aber ich darf nicht. Er sagt, er **sei** um 12 Uhr zu Hause gewesen.

Word type	Various forms		Examples
Nouns	*Case*	*Nominative*	Mein Bruder hat fünf Kinder.
		Accusative	Ich besuche meinen Bruder.
		Dative	Ich helfe meinem Bruder.
		Genitive	Ich mag die Kinder meines Bruders.
	Number	*Singular*	Dieser Film ist langweilig.
		Plural	Ich habe zwei tolle Filme gesehen.
Adjectives	*Compari-son*	*Positive*	Das ist ein gut**er** Film.
		Comparative	Sein letzter Film war aber **besser**.
		Superlative	**Am besten** hat mir sein erster Film gefallen.

Word formation

6 Introduction

In every "living" language, new words are constantly being created. Usually, a word that already exists is altered or combined with another one to form a compound word. Here you can see several different ways of forming words in German.

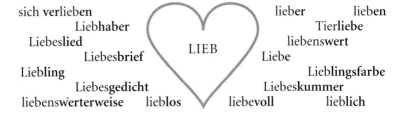

sich **verlieben**
Lieb**haber**
Liebeslied
Liebesbrief
Liebling
Liebesgedicht
liebens**werterweise**   lieb**los**

LIEB

lieber   lieben
Tier**liebe**
liebens**wert**
Liebe
Lieblings**farbe**
Liebeskummer
liebe**voll**   lieb**lich**

All these words belong to one word family, but are different word types:

Verbs	lieben, sich verlieben
Adjectives	liebevoll, liebenswert …
Nouns	die Liebe, der Liebhaber, die Lieblingsfarbe …

If you already know one word in a word family, it is a lot easier to understand and remember other words from the same family.

There are two ways of forming new words:

1. Derivatives – eg prefixes, suffixes   sich **verlieben**, liebe**voll** …

                                      ↓   ↓

                                 Prefix   *Suffix*

2. Compound words   der Liebes**brief**, der Liebes**kummer** …
                            himmel**blau**, mit**kommen**

The last part of a compound word shows what type of word the new word is. The last word is the base word. The meaning of the base word is given a more precise definition by the words put in front of it.

mit *(preposition)* + kommen *(verb)* = mitkommen *(verb)*

When nouns are put together, the new word has the same gender (and, therefore, the same article) as the last word in the noun (the base word).

die Liebe *(feminine)* + der Brief *(masculine)* = der Liebesbrief *(masculine)*

7   Word formation: nouns

Suffixes can be used to make nouns out of other word types, or to change the meaning of a noun.

You can tell which article to use by the suffix:

1 Nouns with the suffixes -ung, -heit,- keit, -schaft are always feminine.	-ung	anmelden	die Anmeldung
	-heit	krank	die Krankheit
		frei	die Freiheit
	-keit	dankbar	die Dankbarkeit
		höflich	die Höflichkeit
	-schaft	der Freund	die Freundschaft

2 Nouns with the suffix -er are always masculine.	-er	backen	der Bäcker	+ *umlaut* a → ä
		arbeiten	der Arbeiter	

3 Nouns with the suffix -in denote a female person.	-in	der Bäcker	die Bäckerin	
		der Arzt	die Ärztin	+ *umlaut* a → ä

4 Nouns with the suffixes -chen, -lein are diminutives
and are always neuter:

der Mann	das Männchen/Männlein	+ *umlaut* a → ä
das Haus	das Häuschen/Häuslein	+ *umlaut* a → ä
die Blume	das Blümchen/Blümlein	+ *umlaut* u → ü

5 Diminutive forms are often used as pet names:

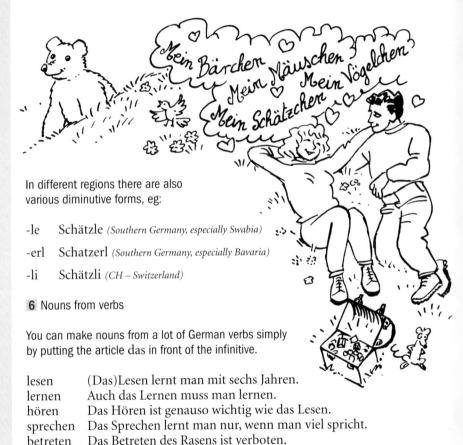

In different regions there are also
various diminutive forms, eg:

-le   Schätzle *(Southern Germany, especially Swabia)*

-erl   Schatzerl *(Southern Germany, especially Bavaria)*

-li   Schätzli *(CH – Switzerland)*

6 Nouns from verbs

You can make nouns from a lot of German verbs simply
by putting the article das in front of the infinitive.

lesen	(Das)Lesen lernt man mit sechs Jahren.
lernen	Auch das Lernen muss man lernen.
hören	Das Hören ist genauso wichtig wie das Lesen.
sprechen	Das Sprechen lernt man nur, wenn man viel spricht.
betreten	Das Betreten des Rasens ist verboten.

In German, nouns can be combined with almost all other word types to make new nouns.
Sometimes an -s-, -e- or -n- is put between the original words to help make the
pronunciation easier. Alternatively, certain letters are sometimes dropped.

der Einkaufszettel	der Einkauf *(noun)*	+	der Zettel *(noun)*
der Fernsehapparat	fernsehen *(verb)*	+	der Apparat *(noun)*
der Mitarbeiter	mit *(preposition)*	+	der Arbeiter *(noun)*
das Klassenzimmer	die Klasse *(noun)*	+	das Zimmer *(noun)*
die Landkarte	das Land *(noun)*	+	die Karte *(noun)*
die Großstadt	groß *(adjective)*	+	die Stadt *(noun)*

The defining word adds a piece of information to the base word.
The base word determines the article.
(For more information about nouns → 📖 **C 28–37.**)

8 Word formation: adjectives

A lot of adjectives are derived from nouns or verbs.
You can recognize an adjective by its ending (or suffix). Here are some frequently used suffixes:

-bar	lesbar, hörbar (Man kann etwas lesen, hören.)
-ig /- isch / -lich	kräftig, modisch, veränderlich (Wie jemand/etwas ist.)
-sam	sparsam, aufmerksam (Wie jemand/etwas ist.)

Here is an example of a prefix (the opposite of suffix). The prefix **un-** often indicates the opposite of the base word:

un-	unbezahlbar	(Man kann es nicht bezahlen.)
	unglücklich	(Nicht glücklich.)
	unveränderlich	(Man kann es nicht verändern.)
	unmöglich	(Es ist nicht möglich.)

There are a number of words that can act as suffixes. These words are often used to form adjectives from other word types as well. Here are a few examples:

Suffix	Example	Equivalent
-los	arbeitslos	Rudolf ist **ohne** Arbeit.
-frei	alkoholfrei	Das Bier ist **ohne** Alkohol.
-arm	fettarm	Der Käse hat **wenig** Fett, nur 20%.
-reich	verkehrsreich	Die Straße hat **viel** Verkehr.
-voll	hoffnungsvoll	Ich gehe mit **viel** Hoffnung in die Prüfung.
-wert	sehenswert	Man sollte den Film ansehen.
-fest	feuerfest	Es kann nicht brennen.

Adjectives are often combined with nouns to describe them more specifically.

schneeweiß   Sie trug ein schneeweißes Hochzeitskleid.
rosarot   Sie ist Optimistin. Sie sieht alles durch die rosarote Brille.
bärenstark   Der Film war super, echt bärenstark!
haushoch   Wir haben das Spiel haushoch verloren, 8 zu 0.
bettelarm   Er hat alles verloren, er ist bettelarm.

9   Word formation: verbs

Many verbs are formed by adding prefixes to a base verb. Many prefixes were originally prepositions (→ 📖 C 77–83) or adverbs (→ 📖 C 90–91).
These prefixes can give the base verb a completely new meaning.

Some verbs have prefixes that can be separated from the verb (separable verbs) and others have inseparable prefixes (inseparable verbs). (→ 📖 C 25)

When learning a verb, you not only have to learn the meaning of the verb, which in most cases can not be deduced from the separate parts (prefix and base verb), but you also have to note whether or not the prefix can be separated from the verb.

Here is one example of a separable verb, with three of its meanings:

anmachen   Als er das Radio anmachte, hörte er sein Lieblingslied „Michelle".
Um Salat anzumachen, verwende ich nur Essig, Öl, Salz und Zucker.
In letzter Zeit machen immer häufiger die Frauen auch die Männer an.

Verbs

10   What do we use verbs for?

The words in bold print in the following text are verbs.

Ich **heiße** Helmut Kohl. Das **ist** meine Frau. Sie **heißt** Hannelore. Ich **komme** aus Ludwigshafen. Das **liegt** im Bundesland Rheinland-Pfalz. Meine Frau **kocht** gern und ich **esse** gern. Meine Frau und ich **haben** ein Kochbuch **geschrieben**. Es **heißt** „Kulinarische Reise durch deutsche Lande".

In **eurolingua** we mark verbs as follows: ⬭

With a verb you can describe

things that people do: Ich (esse) gern.

a state: Ich (heiße) Helmut. Das (ist) Hannelore.

Wir (haben) ein Kochbuch (geschrieben).

The form of the verb says
something about the person
doing the action: Ich heiße Helmut.

… and when the action is
carried out (or tense): Wir **haben** ein Kochbuch **geschrieben.**

11 The infinitive

In dictionaries, you will find
verbs in their infinitive form.
Almost all infinitives in German end in -en.
(→ 📖 C 22)
The only exceptions are the
verbs sein (to be), tun
(to do) and the verbs
ending in -ern and -eln.

kommen 1 come* Kommen Sie bitte her. Come here,
please. Die Kinder kamen ins Zimmer gerannt. The
children came running into the room. Woher kommen
Sie? Where do you come from?
2 (*erreichen*) get* to Am ersten Tag sind wir bis Bath
gekommen. On the first day we got as far as Bath. Wir
sind bis zum letzten Kapitel gekommen. We've got up to
the last chapter.
3 jdn/etwas kommen lassen send* for sb/sth Ich ließ
ein Taxi kommen. I ordered a taxi.

12 Conjugation

In the text in section 10, the
following verb forms exist:

	Infinitive
Ich **heiße** …	heißen
Das **ist** …	sein
Das **liegt** …	liegen
Meine Frau **kocht** …	kochen
Wir **haben** … **geschrieben** …	schreiben

Verbs are used in different forms. Changes to the form of a verb are its conjugation.

13 Stem and ending

Verbs consist of two parts: the stem and various endings.

komm en
↓   ↓
stem   *ending*

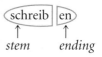

stem   *ending*

The stem shows you what the verb means:

The various endings tell us who, or what, is doing something:

Different persons often have the same verb ending:

er kommt – ihr kommt
wir kochen – sie kochen

The verb endings alone, therefore, do not tell us exactly who, or what, is doing something. For this we need additional words (meine Frau, ich, das Buch …):
Nouns → 📖 C 28–37. Articles, pronouns and determiners → 📖 C 38–61.

14 Person, singular and plural

When conjugating a verb, we differentiate between three persons in the singular and three in the plural.

1st person: ich – wir
You use the first person to refer to yourself (singular) or to yourself and others (plural).

1st person singular

1st person plural

2nd person: du – ihr
You use the second person to refer to the person (singular) or people (plural) you are talking to.
⚠ (→ 📖 C 15).

2nd person singular

2nd person plural

3rd person: er/es/sie – sie
You use the third person to refer to the person (singular) or people (plural) you are talking about.

Sie heißt Claudine.
Er heißt Bernard.

Sie heißen Chaptal.

3rd person singular *3rd person plural*

15 Formal address

In German, when you want to show respect to the person you are talking to, you use the Sie form (siezen).

Formal address always requires the use of the third person plural.

Heißen Sie Helmut Kohl?

Kommen Sie aus Ludwigshafen?

In this case, the pronouns (Sie, Ihnen, etc) always begin with a capital letter.

16 Regular verbs

When a regular verb is conjugated, the stem stays the same in all persons and tenses.

Infinitive:

wohn en

stem ending

Present	*Simple past*	*Perfect*
ich wohne	ich wohnte	ich habe gewohnt
du wohnst	du wohntest	du hast gewohnt
er/sie/es wohnt	er/sie/es wohnte	er/sie/es hat gewohnt
wir wohnen	wir wohnten	wir haben gewohnt
ihr wohnt	ihr wohntet	ihr habt gewohnt
sie wohnen	sie wohnten	sie haben gewohnt

17 Irregular verbs

When an irregular verb is conjugated, the stem also changes for some of the verb forms. It is, therefore, important to learn the various stem forms of these verbs as well.

Present	*Simple past*	*Perfect*
ich **spreche**	ich **sprach**	ich habe ge**sprochen**
du **sprichst**	du **sprachst**	du hast ge**sprochen**
er/sie/es **spricht**	er/sie/es **sprach**	er/sie/es hat ge**sprochen**
wir **sprechen**	wir **sprachen**	wir haben ge**sprochen**
ihr **sprecht**	ihr **spracht**	ihr habt ge**sprochen**
sie **sprechen**	sie **sprachen**	sie haben ge**sprochen**

sprechen
er spricht
er sprach
er hat gesprochen

kommen
er kommt
er kam
er ist gekommen

schreiben
er schreibt
er schrieb
er hat geschrieben

You will find a list of the most important irregular verbs on pages 207–210.

18 Time and tenses

Ich heiße Mehmet Güler. Ich wohne seit 1985 in Stuttgart. Vorher habe ich in Kassel gelebt. Mein Vater war Bauer bei Sorgun in der Türkei. In zehn Jahren gehe ich in die Türkei zurück. Meine Tochter ist in Deutschland geboren. Sie wird hier bleiben.

Mehmet Güler talks about

the past	Vorher habe ich in Kassel gelebt.
	Mein Vater war Bauer ...
the present	Ich wohne seit 1985 in Stuttgart.
and the future	In zehn Jahren gehe ich in die Türkei zurück.
	Sie wird hier bleiben.

In doing this he uses four different tenses:

Perfect	habe ... gelebt
Simple past	war
Present	wohne
	gehe ... zurück
Future	wird ... hier bleiben

In **eurolingua**, you will become acquainted with these four tenses as well as with the fifth form, the pluperfect (or past perfect):

Nachdem Mehmet Güler viele Jahre in Kassel (gelebt) (hatte), ging er 1985 nach Stuttgart.

19 The tenses of regular and irregular verbs

19.1 Present

1 With the present tense you can talk about

the current situation or what is happening now:	Ich wohne in Stuttgart.
	Fabiane liest gerade den Text vor.
something that started earlier, but which is still going on:	Ich lerne seit Januar Deutsch.
	Er liebt sie seit der Schulzeit.
what will happen in the future:	Ich fahre nächstes Jahr nach Brasilien.
something that is always true:	Er heißt Mehmet.
	Er kommt aus der Türkei.

2 The present tense of regular verbs

	Singular ⟨wohn│en⟩ Plural	
1st person	ich wohn e	wir wohn en
2nd person	du wohn st	ihr wohn t
3rd person	er/sie/es wohn t	sie wohn en
Formal address		Sie wohn en

(→ 📖 **C 15**)

⚠ To make pronunciation easier, letters are sometimes added or left out in certain verb forms. Here are three examples:

	(+ e)	(– s)	(– e)
ich	arbeite	heiße	sammle
du	arbeitest	heißt	sammelst
er/es/sie	arbeitet	heißt	sammelt
wir	arbeiten	heißen	sammeln
ihr	arbeitet	heißt	sammelt
sie/Sie	arbeiten	heißen	sammeln

3 The present tense of irregular verbs

The stem of the second and third person singular of many irregular verbs (but not all) is different from the infinitive. You will have to learn the third person singular form for these verbs. (→ 📖 **C 17**)

Infinitive	Present	Simple past	Perfect
fahren	er fährt	er fuhr	er ist gefahren
nehmen	er nimmt	er nahm	er hat genommen
lesen	er liest	er las	er hat gele~~

The endings are the same as for regular verbs.

⚠ The verbs haben, sein, wissen and the modal verbs (dürfen, müssen, können, sollen, wollen) have even more irregular forms.
(→ 📖 **C 27**)

19.2 Use of the tenses for the past: simple past and perfect

Compare the following sentences.

▶ Eine Million Menschen tanzten bei der „Love-Parade" in Berlin.

Gestern **habe** ich die ganze Nacht **getanzt**. Die „Love-Parade" **war** einfach spitze!

Both the simple past and the perfect describe something that was, or something that happened at a time before the moment in which you are speaking.
Both tenses have the same meaning.
They have no one-to-one correspondence with the simple past and perfect in English. In spoken German and also in personal letters, the perfect is often used, whereas in written texts (newspaper articles, literature, etc), the simple past is generally used instead.

Es war einmal ein Mädchen. Das hieß Rotkäppchen. Eines Tages sagte seine Mutter

The verbs haben, sein, wissen and the modal verbs are almost always used in the simple past.

Ich **war** gestern in der Stadt und **wollte** ein Geschenk kaufen. Ich **habe** auch etwas gefunden, aber dann **hatte** ich kein Geld dabei und **musste** ohne Geschenk wieder nach Hause fahren.

19.3 Forming the simple past: regular verbs

The simple past (also known as the imperfect or preterite) is formed in the following way for regular verbs: infinitive stem + simple past ending.

ich	frag **te**	wir	frag **ten**
du	frag **test***	ihr	frag **tet***
er/es/sie	frag **te**	sie	frag **ten**

*The second persons singular and plural are used almost exclusively with a modal verb, or with sein or haben.

⚠ To facilitate pronunciation, an e is inserted between the stem and the ending in verbs with stems ending in -t or -d: arbeit **e** te.

19.4 Forming the simple past: irregular verbs

Irregular verbs almost always have a different stem in the simple past as they do in the infinitive. The stem should, therefore, always be learned along with the infinitive. (→ 📖 C 17).

<u>Infinitive</u>	<u>3rd person: present</u>	<u>3rd person: simple past</u>
sprechen	er spricht	er sprach

Irregular verbs also have their own simple past endings.

Simple past stem (eg ging-) + *ending*

ich	ging **–**	wir	ging **en**
du	ging **st**	ihr	ging **t**
er/es/sie	ging **en**	sie	ging **en**

Several irregular verbs have the same simple past endings as the regular verbs. Haben, wissen and the modal verbs (dürfen, können, müssen …) belong to this group. (→ 📖 C 19.3)

Infinitive	*Present*	*Simple past*	*Perfect*
denken	er denkt	er dachte	er hat gedacht
kennen	er kennt	er kannte	er hat gekannt

Simple past stem (eg dach-) + *simple past ending*

ich	dach **te**	wir	dach **ten**
du	dach **test**	ihr	dach **tet**
er/sie/es	dach **te**	sie	dach **ten**

19.5 Forming the perfect

The perfect is formed in the following way: the present tense of the verb haben or sein + the past participle of the verb.

haben   *past participle:* **lernen**   sein   *past participle:* **gehen**

Ich **habe** gestern eine Stunde **gelernt**, dann **bin** ich in den Kurs **gegangen**.

For more information about forming the past participle → 📖 C 24.
For more information about use of the perfect → 📖 19.2.

1 Perfect tense with haben

Most verbs form the perfect tense with haben:	Ich **habe gefragt.**
	Du **hast geantwortet.**
	Sie **hat abgeschrieben.**
	Wir **haben vorgelesen.**
	Ihr **habt diskutiert.**
	Sie **haben gehandelt.**

2 Perfect tense with sein

Several verbs form the perfect tense with sein:

1. The verbs

bleiben	Ich **bin** gestern zu Hause **geblieben.**
sein	Theo **ist** allein in der Firma **gewesen.**
werden	Er **ist** fast verrückt **geworden.**

2. Several impersonal verbs, such as:

passieren	**Ist** ihm etwas **passiert?**
geschehen	Nein, es **ist** ihm nichts **geschehen.**

3. Verbs that express a change in state or a motion from one place to another.

Er **ist** mit dem Auto **gefahren**.

Er **ist eingeschlafen**.

⚠ Er **hat** sein Auto **kaputtgefahren**.

3 Perfect tense with modal verbs

The perfect tense for modal verbs is formed in two ways:

1. The modal verb is not the main verb:
   If the verb before the modal verb is in the infinitive, the modal verb must also be in the infinitive.

Ich **habe** dich gestern nicht **besuchen können**.

2. The modal verb is the main verb:
   If the modal verb is used without a second verb, the perfect tense is formed using the past participle of the modal verb.

Das **habe** ich nicht **gewollt**.

19.6   **Using and forming the pluperfect (or past perfect)**

Als Tom in die Küche kam, fraß Bello gerade das Hähnchen.

Als Tom in die Küche kam, **hatte** Bello das Hähnchen **gefressen**.

The pluperfect is used in conjunction with the simple past – often in the same sentence. It reveals that the action in the pluperfect happened before the action in the simple past.

Nachdem Tom etwas Brot **gegessen hatte**, **fuhr** er schnell zum Bahnhof.

The pluperfect can also be used alone in a sentence:
Der Hund **hatte** das ganze Hähnchen **gefressen**.

The pluperfect is formed in the following way:
the simple past from haben/sein + the past participle of the main verb.
(For more information about forming the past participle → 📖 C 24.)

Haben or **sein**? The same rules apply as for forming the perfect tense. (→ 📖 C 19.5)

Als Tom auf dem Bahnhof ankam, **war** der Zug schon **abgefahren**.

The pluperfect and modal verbs? The same rules apply as for the perfect tense. (→ 📖 C 19.5)

19.7 The future: future tense and present tense

The future tense is used to talk about what will happen in the future.
It is most often used when making predictions (eg about the weather), or when talking about plans, intentions and promises for the future.

Intention	Ab morgen **werde** ich weniger **arbeiten** und mehr Sport **machen**.
Prediction	Im Jahr 2525 **werden** die Menschen nur noch montags **arbeiten**.
Promise	Nächstes Jahr **werden** wir dich ganz bestimmt öfter **besuchen**.

However, the present tense is often used (together with a given time reference) instead of the future tense:

Ich fahre morgen nach Berlin.
Ab Oktober arbeite ich nur noch 35 Stunden.
Ich besuche dich morgen.

The future tense can also be used to fomulate speculations and demands.

Speculation	Er wird wohl jetzt zu Hause sein.
Demand	Du wirst mir jetzt sofort mein Geld zurückgeben!

The future tense is formed in the following way:
present tense of werden + infinitive of the main verb.

Conjugation of werden:	ich werde	wir werden
	du wirst	ihr werdet
	. er/es/sie wird	sie werden

In German, there is another future form: the future perfect. It is used to talk about an event or action which will be in the past, at a given time in the future (the past of the future). It is rarely used in German and is not used in **eurolingua Deutsch**. Here are two examples, so you know what it looks like:

Prediction   Im Jahre 2525 **werden** die Menschen alle Krankheiten **besiegt haben.**

Speculation   Er **wird** den Zug **verpasst haben.**

19.8   **Summary: times and tenses**

Time	Tense	Examples
Past	*Pluperfect* (→ 📖 C 19.6)	Nachdem Eva Tom **angerufen hatte,** fuhr sie zu Paul. Nachdem sie **weggegangen war**, rief Tom noch mal an.
	Simple past (→ 📖 C 19.3, C 19.4)	Sie **liebte** Tom, aber sie **hatte** auch Paul gern.
	Perfect (→ 📖 C 19.5)	Tom: Ich **hab** dich gestern noch mal **angerufen.** Eva: Ich **bin** nach unserem Gespräch gleich in die Stadt **gefahren.**
Present	*Present* (→ 📖 C 19.1)	Tom: Was **machst** du gerade? Eva: Ich **höre** die neue CD von Nina Hagen. Sie ist super!
Future	*Present* (→ 📖 C 19.1, C 19.7)	Tom: **Kommst** du **morgen**? Eva: **Morgen habe** ich keine Zeit.
	Future (→ 📖 C 19.7)	Tom: Im neuen Jahr **werde** ich alles anders **machen.** (Intention/plan) Eva: Das **wirst** du wohl nicht **schaffen.** (Speculation)

20.1   Indicative

The indicative is used to state what is, what has happened, or what will happen.

> Ich **kann** mir auch nicht erklären, wie es **passiert ist**. Der Hund **hat** mich immer **provoziert** und plötzlich **habe** ich das Gefühl **gehabt**, dass ich ihm eine Lehre erteilen muss.

Briefträger beißt Hund: 200 Euro Geldstrafe

(Verb forms in the indicative → 📖 C 11–19)

20.2   *Konjunktiv I* (Subjunctive I)

1 Use

The *Konjunktiv I* is used in reported speech (or indirect speech).
The *Konjunktiv I* appears almost exclusively in written texts (eg newspaper reports).
It is enough to be able to recognize this form and understand it when you read it.

The verbs that are marked in the following text are in the *Konjunktiv I* form.

Der Briefträger sagte vor Gericht aus, er **könne** sich auch nicht erklären, wie es zur Tat gekommen **sei**. Der Hund **habe** ihn seit Jahren provoziert und plötzlich **habe** er das Gefühl gehabt, er **müsse** dem Hund eine Lehre erteilen. Er **habe** den Hund spontan hinter dem Kopf gepackt und ihm ins Ohr gebissen.

2 *Konjunktiv I*: present tense

The present tense of the *Konjunktiv I* is formed as follows:
infinitive stem + *Konjunktiv I* ending.
The verb sein is an exception.

Infinitive stem + Konjunktiv I ending   *Exception*

(**komm** | en)   (**könn** | en)   (**hab** | en)   (**sein**)

	komm	könn	hab	sein
ich	komm e	könn e	hab e	sei -
du	komm est	könn est	hab est	sei (e)st
er/es/sie	komm e	könn e	hab e	sei -
wir	komm en	könn en	hab en	sei en
ihr	komm et	könn et	hab et	sei et
sie	komm en	könn en	hab en	sei en

Several verb forms in the *Konjunktiv I* are identical to those in the indicative.
In these cases, they are replaced with the *Konjunktiv II* forms.
(*Konjunktiv II* → 📖 **C 20**)
(Reported speech → 📖 **103**)

3 *Konjunktiv I*: perfect tense

This is formed as follows: the *Konjunktiv I* form of haben or sein + the past participle of the main verb.

(haben or sein? → 📖 **C 19.5**)
(Past participle → 📖 **C 24**)

> Der Briefträger betonte, er **habe** die Hundebesitzerin mehrfach **gewarnt,** aber sie **sei** immer sehr unfreundlich **gewesen.**

20.3 Use of the *Konjunktiv II* (Subjunctive II)

You can use the *Konjunktiv II* to:
– talk about things that do not exist / things that you wish for,
– express a wish politely,
– report what someone else has said.

(Forming the *Konjunktiv II* → 📖 **C 20.4**)

Wenn ich Geld **hätte, würde** ich ein Jahr um die Welt **reisen.**
Ich **hätte** gern ein Kilo Kartoffeln.
Er sagte, die Leute **müssten** besser auf ihre Hunde aufpassen.

1 Talking about things that do not exist

Wishes
(→ 📖 B 3)

Ich wäre gern der Hund.
Ich hätte gern einen Hund.
Ich würde die Frau gern kennen
lernen. Ich hätte als Kind auch
gern einen Hund gehabt.

Conditions

Wenn ich einen Hund hätte, wäre ich glücklich.
Wenn das Wetter schön wäre, würde ich eine Fahrradtour machen.

Comparisons

Er tut so, als ob er von nichts wüsste.
Sie arbeitet, als ob es nichts anderes auf der Welt gäbe.

2 Politeness

You can use the *Konjunktiv II* to formulate requests and advice in an especially polite way.

⚠ When speaking, intonation, gestures and
facial expressions are more important than
grammatical forms, in order to express
yourself politely.

Würden Sie
mir bitte noch ein
Bier bringen?!?

Requests

Würdest du mir dein Lernerhandbuch leihen?
Könnten Sie diesen Brief bitte bis morgen schreiben?
Dürfte ich Sie vielleicht morgen noch einmal anrufen?
Hätten Sie etwas Salz und Pfeffer für mich?

Advice

Du solltest nicht so viel arbeiten.
Wenn du dich erholen willst, könntest du in Österreich wandern gehen.
Wäre es nicht besser, wenn ihr mit der Bahn in Urlaub fahren würdet?
(→ 📖 B 8.1)

3 Reported speech

The *Konjunktiv II* is used instead of the *Konjunktiv I*, if the *Konjunktiv I* form is identical to the indicative form.

Indicative = *Konjunktiv I*

Er sagte, die Leute müssen besser auf ihre Hunde aufpassen.

Er sagte, die Leute müssten besser auf ihre Hunde aufpassen.

Konjunktiv II

(→ 📖 C 20.4, C 103)

20.4 Forming the *Konjunktiv II*

1 The present form of the *Konjunktiv II* using würde + infinitive

The *Konjunktiv II* of most verbs is formed using würde + the infinitive.

You should learn to use this form actively, because it is often used in German and is, therefore, very useful.

Ich **würde** jetzt am liebsten vier Wochen ans Meer **fahren.**

Da **würde** ich gleich **mitkommen.**

2 Verbs forms of the *Konjunktiv II*

Sein, haben, werden, wissen and all the modal verbs are used in the *Konjunktiv II* form. They are derived from the simple past. You should learn to use these forms actively:

Simple past	er/es/sie	wusste	wurde	hatte	war	konnte
Konjunktiv II	ich	wüsste	würde	hätte	wäre	könnte
	du	wüsstest	würdest	hättest	wärst	könntest
	er/es/sie	wüsste	würde	hätte	wäre	könnte
	wir	wüssten	würden	hätten	wären	könnten
	ihr	wüsstet	würdet	hättet	wärt	könntet
	sie	wüssten	würden	hätten	wären	könnten

All other verbs have *Konjunktiv II* forms too, but they are seldom used nowadays.

3 *Konjunktiv II*: perfect tense

The perfect tense of the *Konjunktiv II* is formed in the following way:
Konjunktiv II present tense of haben/sein + past participle of the main verb.

Wenn du die Zeitung **gelesen hättest, hättest** du **gewusst,** dass das Konzert ausfällt.
Ich **wäre** traurig **gewesen,** wenn du nicht **gekommen wärst.**

(haben or sein? → 📖 **19.5**)
(Past participle → 📖 **24**)

20.5 Imperative

You can use the imperative to

Geben Sie mir bitte mal den Taschenrechner.

Geh doch öfter mal schwimmen.

formulate requests

give advice

Seid endlich ruhig und lest den Text!

Rauchen Sie nicht und benutzen Sie keine elektronischen Geräte!

give instructions

express prohibition

(Imperatives → 📖 **C 99**)

1 Forming the imperative

The imperative has three forms:

2nd person singular
Like the 2nd person singular
of the present tense, but
without st and without du.

(du) mach(st)

Mach bitte das Licht aus.

3rd person plural
Like the 3rd person plural
of the present tense, except that
Sie comes after the verb.

Sie gehen

Gehen Sie nach Hause.

2nd person plural
Like the 2nd person plural
of the present tense, but without
ihr.

(ihr) schaltet

Schaltet bitte alle Lichter aus.

2 Special cases

	du	ihr	Sie
haben	Hab keine Angst.		
sein	Sei ruhig!	Seid höflich.	Seien Sie vorsichtig!
werden	Werd(e) gesund.		

Several irregular verbs which usually have a vowel change in the stem in the indicative keep the original vowel from the infinitive stem in the imperative.

laufen	Lauf schneller.
fahren	Fahr vorsichtig.
schlafen	Schlaf jetzt!

Verbs ending in -eln and -ern

klingeln	Klingle zweimal.
ändern	Ändere das Passwort!

(Imperatives of separable verbs → 📖 C 25.1)

Orders, advice, etc can also be expressed using other grammatical forms.
(→ 📖 B 8.1, 24)

1 Use

Ein Arbeiter baut den Motor in das Auto.	Der Motor **wird** in das Auto **eingebaut**.

The passive is used to talk about what is done with/to something. It is not important to say who is responsible for the action. The "doer" is not as important as the action itself.

The passive is often found in factual writing (eg instruction manuals, descriptions of manufacturing processes, newpaper reports ...).

If you want to refer to the doer of the action in a passive sentence, you use von + the dative:

Früher wurde ein Auto **von** vielen Arbeitern gebaut.
Heute wird ein Auto fast komplett **von** einem Roboter gebaut.

2 Forming the passive

Werden (conjugated) + the past participle of the main verb.

Indicative	*Present*	Das Auto wird gebaut.
	Perfect	Das Auto ist gebaut worden.
	Simple past	Das Auto wurde gebaut.
	Pluperfect	Das Auto war gebaut worden.
	Future	Das Auto wird gebaut werden.
Konjunktiv I	*Present*	Er sagte, das Auto werde gebaut.
	Perfect	Er sagte, das Auto sei gebaut worden.
Konjunktiv II	*Present*	Das Auto würde gebaut, wenn ...
	Perfect	Das Auto wäre gebaut worden.

3 The passive with modal verbs

The passive with modals verbs is formed in the following way:

Modal verb conjugated + past participle of main verb + werden

Die unregelmäßigen Verben **müssen** regelmäßig **wiederholt werden**.

Früher **mussten** Autos ganz von Hand **gebaut werden**.

In Zukunft **sollte** viel mehr mit dem Fahrrad **gefahren werden**.

4 The passive in subordinate clauses

The whole verb phrase comes at the end of the subordinate clause.

Man entwickelte Autos, nachdem der Motor **erfunden worden war**.
Uhren waren früher viel teurer, weil sie von Hand **gebaut wurden**.
Ich weiß, dass die unregelmäßigen Verben oft **wiederholt werden müssen**.
Ich frage mich, ob in 200 Jahren noch Autos **gebaut werden**.

22 Infinitives

The infinitive is the basic form of a verb. This is the form you will find in a dictionary.

Almost all verbs end in -en in the infinitive.

Two verbs end in -n: sein, tun, and several verbs have the endings -eln and -ern in the infinitive: erinnern, lächeln, klingeln …

spie·len; *spielte, hat gespielt;* [Vt] **1** *(etw.)* **s.** ein (bestimmtes) Spiel (1,2,3) machen ⟨Fangen, Verstecken, Räuber u. Gendarm s.; Mühle, Dame, Mikado, Karten, Skat, Schafkopf, Schach usw s.; beim Spielen schwindeln⟩: *mit Puppen s.; mit den Kindern im Garten Federball s.* **2** *(etw.)* **s.** etw. regelmäßig als Sport od. Hobby tun ⟨Fußball, (Tisch)Tennis, Volleyball, Minigolf s.⟩: *Der Stürmer ist verletzt u. kann heute nicht s.* **3** *(etw.)* **s.** Musik machen ⟨ein Instrument s.; Klavier, Geige, Flöte s.; ein Musikstück s.; e-e Sinfonie, ein Lied, e-n Marsch s.⟩ **4** *(etw.)* **s.** (beim Roulette, an Automaten usw) versuchen, Geld zu gewinnen ⟨Roulette, Lotto, Toto s.; mit hohen Einsätzen s.⟩ ‖ K-: **spiel-, -süchtig 5** *(j-n l etw.)* **s.** (als Schauspieler) e-e Person / Rolle in e-m Film od. Theaterstück darstellen ⟨die Hauptrolle, e-e Nebenrolle s.⟩: *in Goethes „Faust" den Mephisto s.; Spielt er in diesem Film?*; [Vi] **6** ⟨e-e Theatergruppe o. ä.⟩ *spielt etw.* e-e Theatergruppe o. ä. zeigt e-e künstlerische Produktion dem Publikum, führt etw. auf ⟨ein Theaterstück, e-e Oper, ein Musical, e-n Film usw s.⟩: *Das Stadttheater spielt diesen Winter „Die Räuber" von Schiller* **7** *etw.* **s.** oft pej; so tun, als ob man etw. wäre, was man in Wirklichkeit nicht ist ⟨den Clown, den Boß, die Starke, die f'ı...

From: Langenscheidts Großwörterbuch
Deutsch als Fremdsprache

22.1 The infinitive without zu

The following texts say how to do something or what not to do.

Und so wird's gemacht:

1. Wasserbehälter mit frischem Wasser füllen und einsetzen.
2. Betriebsschalter drücken.
3. Filtersieb einlegen und eine Portion Espresso einfüllen.

Apfelmus-Varianten

Apfelmus mit Mandeln und Nüssen. Je 2 Essl. Mandeln und Haselnüsse in einer trockenen Bratpfanne hellgelb rösten. 1 Essl. Rosinen ½ Stunde in Rum oder Cognac einlegen. Vor dem Servieren alles über das Apfelmus verteilen. Mit 2 Essl. Zimtzucker bestreuen und mit kühlem, steifgeschlagenem Rahm servieren.

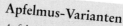

Spielen der Kinder auf dem Hof verboten

The infinitive is used, for example:

in demands/requests instructions: (→ 📖 B 24)	Bitte anschnallen und das Rauchen einstellen. Nicht rauchen. Nicht Ball spielen. Die Suppe leicht kochen. Kartoffeln schälen.
in the compound tenses: *Future* *Konjunktiv II*	Morgen **wird** es kalt **werden**. Ich **würde** gern in den Süden **fahren**.
with modal verbs:	Du **musst** morgen einen Mantel **anziehen**. Es **soll** sehr kalt **werden**.

with the following verbs:		
	bleiben	Ich **bleibe** im Bett **liegen**.
	gehen	Ich **gehe** nicht **spazieren**.
	hören	Ich **höre** den Wind an den Bäumen **rütteln**.
	kommen	Schneewolken **kommen geflogen**.
	sehen	Ich **sehe** die Vögel nach Süden **fliegen**.
	lassen	Ich **lasse** mir die Haare **wachsen**.
	schicken	Ich **schicke** meinen Sohn **einkaufen**.

All other verbs take the infinitive with zu.

as a noun (→ 📖 C 7)	Vor dem **Schlafen** trinke ich ein Glas Rotwein.

22.2 The infinitive with zu

The infinitive with zu is often used in expressions like the following:

Ich habe (keine) Lust,	Lernkärtchen **zu schreiben.**
Ich habe keine Zeit,	Vokabeln **zu lernen.**
Ich versuche,	mich im Unterricht **zu konzentrieren.**
Ich fange an,	eine Wortschatzkartei **zu führen.**
Hör auf,	dauernd **zu jammern!**
Ich hoffe,	bald in Österreich **zu wohnen.**
Es ist schön,	die Sprache der Leute **zu sprechen.**
Es ist interessant,	neue Menschen **kennen zu lernen.**
Es ist nicht leicht,	aus der Heimat **wegzugehen.**

The infinitive with zu can also come after the following words:

um	Ich arbeite viel, **um** gut **zu leben.**
anstatt	Er arbeitet zu viel, **anstatt** wirklich **zu leben.**
ohne	Sie lebt zufrieden, **ohne** viel **zu arbeiten.**

The infinitive with zu can also come after haben and sein:

haben	Ich **habe** heute noch viel **zu tun.**
	(= Ich **muss** heute noch viel **tun.**)
sein	Herr Wetz **ist** ab 14 Uhr **zu sprechen.**
	(= Man **kann** mit Herrn Wetz ab 14 Uhr **sprechen.**)
	Es ist viel zu tun.
	(= Wir **müssen** viel tun.)

22.3 The infinitive with zu for separable verbs

With separable verbs, the zu is placed between the two parts of the verb.

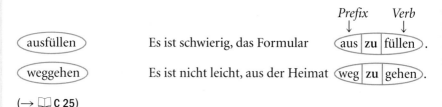

(→ 📖 C 25)

The present participle is formed as follows: infinitive + d. When declining the present participle or using its comparative or superlative forms, the approriate endings are added to the d. (→ 📖 C 65–72)

ein bellender Hund
ein schreiendes Kind
eine miauende Katze
mit hängenden Ohren

The verbs in bold print in the following text are all present participles.

Mond-Tag
Glitzerndes Licht im Wasser des Sees.
Ich höre **rauschende** Blätter im **schweigenden** Wald.
Leuchtende Würmchen fliegen vorbei.
Die **Liebenden** verstecken sich in Sonnenblumen.
Das **schreiende** Mondlicht stört die Nacht.

The present participle is used to assign an action (glitzern – to glitter, lieben – to love) to a noun (Licht – light), or can be used as a noun (die Liebenden) referring to someone or something that does a specific thing (lieben – to love).

„Leuchtende Würmchen" sind Würmchen, die leuchten.
„Liebende" sind Menschen, die sich lieben.
„Rauschende Blätter" sind Blätter, die im Wind rauschen.

The present participles in these sentences are used either as adjectives or nouns. When used as an adjective before a noun and when used as a noun, the present participle is declined as if it were an adjective.
After a noun, the present participle – like adjectives – takes no ending.

Adjective
after the noun   Die Hunde rennen **bellend** aus dem Haus.
before the noun   Ich habe Angst vor bellend**en** Hunden.

Noun
(→ 📖 C 5)   Die **Reisenden** nach Kairo werden zum Flugsteig A 47 gebeten.
Als **Reisende/r** kann man auf Flughäfen einiges erleben.

24 The past participle

The past participle is used to form the following tenses:

Perfect (→ 📖 **C 19.2, 19.5**)	Er **hat** Suppe **gekocht**.
Pluperfect (→ 📖 **C 19.6**)	Als sie nach Hause kam, **hatte** er die Suppe schon **gekocht**.
Passive (→ 📖 **C 21**)	Die Pizza **wird gebracht**.

The past participle as an adjective

– after verbs	Die Pizza ist **verbrannt**.
– after nouns	Die **Pizza** ist mit Salami **belegt**.
– before nouns	**Verbrannte Pizza** schmeckt mir nicht.

When the past participle comes directly before the noun it describes, it is declined like an adjective. (→ 📖 **C 5, C 65–72**)

The past participle of regular verbs is formed as follows:

ge ... t	ge ... et	... t	... ge ... t	... ge ... et
gekauft gelernt	gearbeitet geheiratet	studiert buchstabiert	eingekauft* abgeholt*	eingearbeitet* abgewartet*

*With separable verbs, the ge comes between the two parts of the verb.
(→ 📖 **C 25.1**)

The past participle of irregular verbs is usually formed as follows:

ge + *past participle stem* + en.

gehen	ge | gang | en	Er ist gegangen.
singen	ge | sung | en	Sie hat schön gesungen.
wegfahren	weg | ge | fahr | en	Müllers sind weggefahren.
mitsingen	mit | ge | sung | en	Alle haben mitgesungen.
verstehen	verstanden*	Ich habe alles verstanden.

*The past participle of inseparable verbs is formed without ge.
(→ 📖 **C 25**)

The past participle of irregular verbs has to be learned by heart, just like the simple past forms. (→ 📖 C 19.4)

singen
sang
gesungen

In the list of irregular verbs, you will find the past participle in the fourth column. (→ 📖 Appendix 3)

25   Separable and inseparable verbs

25.1   Separable verbs

Many verbs in German can take a large number of verb prefixes.

schreiben	<u>au</u>fschreiben, <u>a</u>bschreiben, m<u>i</u>tschreiben, <u>vo</u>rschreiben ...
kommen	<u>a</u>nkommen, <u>a</u>bkommen, m<u>i</u>tkommen, <u>u</u>nterkommen ...
lesen	<u>a</u>blesen, m<u>i</u>tlesen, n<u>a</u>chlesen, <u>vo</u>rlesen ...

The prefix often gives the verb a completely different meaning.

Most of these prefixes are stressed. Stressed prefixes are separable. In the conjugated forms of these verbs (in main clauses) the prefixes are always separated.

⬭ vor │ lesen ⬭   Ich ⬭ lese ⬭ jetzt die Teilnehmerliste weiter ⬭ vor ⬭.

⬭ mit │ schreiben ⬭   Schreiben ⬭ Sie den Satz bitte ⬭ mit ⬭.

However, when the conjugated verb comes at the end of a subordinate clause, the prefix is not separated.

⬭ an │ kommen ⬭   Ich glaube nicht, dass er heute ⬭ankommt⬭.

Here is a list of the most important separable verb prefixes:

Prefix	*Infinitive* (Example)	Conjugated form ....
ab-	abfahren	Wann **fährt** der Zug **ab**?
an-	anrufen	**Ruf** mich bitte **an**.
auf-	aufhören	**Hört** doch endlich **auf**!
aus-	ausgehen	**Gehst** du mit mir **aus**?
bei-	beilegen	**Legen** Sie bitte die Rechnung **bei**.
dar-	darstellen	Die Skulptur **stellt** einen Baum **dar**.
ein-	einladen	Ich **lade** dich zur Party **ein**.

fest-	feststellen	Ich **stelle fest**, dass ich kein Geld habe.
fort-	fortlaufen	**Lauf** bitte nicht **fort**!
her-	herkommen	**Komm** mal **her**!
hin-	hinfallen	Mein Kind **fällt** jeden Tag einmal **hin**.
los-	losfahren	Wann **fahren** wir endlich **los**?
mit-	mitkommen	**Kommst** du **mit**?
nach-	nachdenken	Ich **denke** oft über die Menschen **nach**.
nieder-	niederschlagen	James Bond **schlägt** seine Feinde **nieder**.
vor-	vorschlagen	Ich **schlage vor**, dass wir ins Kino gehen.
weg-	wegfahren	Wann **fährst** du **weg**?
weiter-	weiterarbeiten	**Arbeiten** Sie ruhig **weiter**.
zu-	zuhören	**Hör** mal **zu**.
zurück-	zurückkommen	Wann **kommst** du **zurück**?

This is what entries for separable verbs look like in a dictionary:

⌈Lesen⌉ Sie bitte den Text ⌈vor⌉ und ⌈schreiben⌉ Sie die Regel ⌈ab⌉.

vor-ner-stung *ale*; ge....., e-e Leistung od. Arbeit,
bevor *bes* ein Vertrag geschlossen wird: *Keiner der
Verhandlungspartner war zu Vorleistungen bereit*
vor-le-sen *(hat)* Ⓥᵢᵢ *(j-m) (etw.) v.* etw. laut lesen,
damit andere es hören: *den Kindern Märchen v.* ‖
K-: **Vorlese-, -wettbewerb**

-mittel, -politik, -strategie, -waffe
ạb-schrei-ben *(hat)* Ⓥᵢᵢ **1** *(etw.) (von j-m) a.* den
Text e-s anderen übernehmen, kopieren u. ihn als
eigenes Werk ausgeben: *Er schrieb fast den ganzen
Aufsatz vom Nachbarn ab;* Ⓥᵢ **2** *etw.* **(von / aus**
etw.) a. e-e handschriftliche Kopie von e-m Text

25.2   Inseparable verbs

The following seven verb prefixes are never stressed.
They can not be separated from the verb.

be -	bes<u>u</u>chen, be<u>a</u>ntworten, begr<u>ei</u>fen …
ent-	entd<u>e</u>cken, entl<u>a</u>ssen, entw<u>e</u>rfen …
er-	erz<u>ä</u>hlen, erf<u>i</u>nden, ersch<u>a</u>ffen …
ge-	geh<u>ö</u>ren, gef<u>a</u>llen, gest<u>e</u>hen …
ver-	verl<u>ie</u>ben, verl<u>ie</u>ren, verg<u>e</u>ssen …
zer-	zerst<u>ö</u>ren, zerf<u>a</u>llen, zert<u>ei</u>len …
wider-	widerspr<u>e</u>chen, widerst<u>e</u>hen …

⚠ The verb prefix miss- is usually stressed, but is nevertheless inseparable.

| miss- | m<u>i</u>ssverstehen, m<u>i</u>sslingen … |

A few verb prefixes are sometimes stressed and separable and sometimes unstressed and inseparable.

umf<u>a</u>hren   <u>u</u>mfahren

Sie hat den Hund geschickt umf<u>a</u>hren.   Er hat den Hund <u>u</u>mgefahren.

26 Reflexive verbs

Er gefällt ihr.   Er gefällt sich selbst.
Sie hat sich in ihn verliebt.   Er hat sich in sich selbst verliebt.

Many verbs can be used as reflexive verbs. Depending on the verb, the pronoun or noun following it takes either the dative or the accusative. Here are a few examples:

Non-reflexive	Reflexive	Case
helfen Er hilft **mir**.	Ich helfe **mir** selbst.	*Dative*
kaufen Ich kaufe **uns** ein Eis.	Ich kaufe **mir** ein Eis.	*Dative*
ärgern Ärgere **ihn** nicht!	Er ärgert **sich** doch selbst.	*Accusative*
lieben Liebt er **sie**?	Der liebt doch nur **sich** selbst.	*Accusative*

(Reflexive pronouns → 📖 C 57)

Some verbs must always be used with reflexive pronouns. In a dictionary, they will be listed as follows, for example:

aiguidai ...
be'dächtig [bə'dɛçtiç] (vorsichtig) prudente, cauteloso; (langsam) vagaroso
be'danken (sem ge-, h) sich bei j-m für etw agradecer a/c a alg
Be'darf [bə'darf] m (-es; 0) necessidade f; falta f ... ll ... de necessi

sich bedanken	Er bedankt **sich** für die schönen Blumen.
sich entschließen	Ich habe **mich** entschlossen, nach Brasilien zu gehen.
sich verspäten	Ich werde **mich** etwas verspäten.
sich erholen	Unser Urlaub war super. Wir haben **uns** toll erholt.

Verbs with reflexive pronouns can also be used to express a mutual or reciprocal relationship:

sich lieben	Sie lieben sich wie Romeo und Julia. (= They love each other.)
sich hassen	Sie hassen sich bis aufs Blut. (= They hate each other.)
sich verstehen	Wir verstehen uns sehr gut, fast ganz ohne Worte. (= We understand each other.)
sich helfen	Wenn es Probleme gibt, helfen sie sich gegenseitig. (= They help each other.)

27 Verbs with special functions

Several verbs in German have special functions. The most important of these are:

auxiliary verbs	haben, sein
modal verbs	dürfen, können, mögen, müssen, sollen, wollen
the verbs	brauchen, kennen, wissen, lassen, werden

27.1 The auxiliary verbs haben and sein

Haben and sein are often used as auxiliary verbs, that is to say they help to form compound tenses such as the perfect and the pluperfect.
(→ 📖 C 19.5, C 19.6)

Ich **habe** heute 12 Stunden gearbeitet.
Ich **bin** nur 30 Minuten spazieren gegangen.

Haben and sein can also be used as "normal" (or main) verbs.

Ich habe ein Haus, ein großes Auto und viel Geld, aber ich bin nicht glücklich.

Haben and sein are irregular verbs.
You will find their various forms in the list of irregular verbs. (→ 📖 Appendix 3)

What are modal verbs used for?
Look at the following pictures and compare the sentences.

Sie arbeitet nicht. (She does not work / is not working.)

Sie **darf** nicht arbeiten. Sie **kann** nicht arbeiten. Sie **mag** nicht arbeiten.
(She has no work permit.) (She is ill.) (She does not like working.)

Sie **muss** nicht arbeiten. Sie **soll** nicht arbeiten. Sie **will** nicht arbeiten.
(She is on holiday.) (The doctor has advised (She is lazy.)
her not to.)

The verbs that appear in bold print are modal verbs. There are six modal verbs in German:

dürfen, können, mögen, müssen, sollen, wollen

Modal verbs are usually used in conjunction with another verb, the main verb. The second
verb is used in the infinitive.

Ich (muss) morgen (arbeiten).

A modal verb is sometimes used without another main verb, but the main verb is still "understood". In the following examples, the "understood" verb is shown in brackets:

Sie **dürfen** jetzt nach Hause. (gehen)
Er **kann** gut Deutsch. (sprechen)
Ich **mag** jetzt keinen Tee. (trinken)
Ich **muss** morgen nach Leipzig. (fahren)
Ich **will** eine Gehaltserhöhung. (haben)

Modal verb forms: modal verbs are irregular verbs.
You will find their various forms in the list of irregular verbs.
(→ 📖 **Appendix 3**)

What can you express with modal verbs? Here are a few examples:

Modal verb......Example .... Meaning ....

Modal verb	Example	Meaning
dürfen	Du **darfst** den Film sehen.	Permission
dürfen + negation	Du **darfst** den Film **nicht** sehen. Sie **dürfen keinen** Alkohol trinken.	Prohibition
dürfen in the *Konj. II*	Er **dürfte** 23 Jahre alt sein.	Speculation
können	Du **kannst** hier viel lernen. Ich **kann** Gitarre spielen. Sie **können** nach Hause gehen.	Possibility Ability Permission
können + negation	Du **kannst** hier **nichts** lernen. Man **kann** hier **kein** Obst kaufen. Ich **kann nicht** Gitarre spielen. Ich sehe keine Licht. Er **kann** noch **nicht** zu Hause sein.	Impossibility Inability Conclusion
können in the *Konjunktiv II*	Sie **könnte** im Kino sein.	Speculation

Modal verb	Example	Meaning
mögen	Ich **mag** Jazzmusik.* Da **mögen** Sie Recht haben.	Like* Possibility
mögen + negation	Ich **mag** Jazzmusik **nicht**.* Ich **mag nicht** darüber sprechen.	Dislike* Reluctance
mögen in the *Konj. II*	Ich **möchte** einen Ausflug machen. Ich **möchte** ein Kilo Bananen, bitte.	Wish

*When mögen has this meaning it is used alone, without another verb in the infinitive.

müssen	Du **musst** den Salat essen. Es ist schon acht, ich **muss** jetzt gehen. Ich sehe Licht. Er **muss** zu Hause sein.	Order Necessity Conclusion
müssen + negation	Du **musst keinen** Salat essen. Sie **müssen** diese Wörter **nicht** lernen. Es ist erst sechs, ich **muss** noch **nicht** gehen.	Options Lack of necessity

sollen	Du **sollst** jetzt still sein. Ich **soll** Ihnen diesen Brief geben. Das Beispiel **soll** Ihnen helfen. Er **soll** sehr reich sein.	Order Task Purpose Rumour
sollen + negation	Du **sollst nicht** töten. Du **sollst keinen** Kaffee trinken.	Prohibition

wollen	Ich **will** einen Ausflug machen. Er **will** gestern im Kino gewesen sein, aber das glaube ich nicht.	Desire/Wish Doubt
wollen + negation	Ich **will nicht** spazieren gehen.	Refusal

⚠ The modal verb wollen can sound impolite, so other forms are often used to replace it, eg:

Ich will jetzt nach Hause gehen.	(Can sound impolite or unfriendly.)
Ich möchte jetzt nach Hause gehen.	(Sounds more polite and friendly.)

27.3 The verbs brauchen, kennen, wissen, lassen, werden

1 The verb brauchen

The verb brauchen can be used like a modal verb.

As a main verb Ich brauche einen Bleistift.
Brauchst du etwas aus der Stadt?

As a modal verb In diesem Text **brauchen** Sie <u>nicht</u> jedes Wort **zu** verstehen.
Du **brauchst** mich <u>nur</u> anzurufen, ich helfe dir sofort.

When used as a modal verb, brauchen is always used in conjunction with the words nur or nicht, and the main verb is used in the infinitive with zu.

2 The verbs kennen and wissen

Both of these verbs can be translated as "to know" in English.
Kennen can be used to talk about experiences a person has had with other people or things.

Ich kenne das Buch sehr gut.
Wir kennen uns seit 20 Jahren.
Er kennt das Problem.
Ich kenne den Mann nicht, aber ich kenne seine Exfrau.

Wissen can be used to talk about factual information that a person has.

Ich weiß, dass das Buch gut ist.
Ich weiß alles über ihn.
Ich weiß eine Lösung für das Problem.
Er weiß nicht, ob der Termin heute oder morgen ist.
Wissen Sie, wie man zum Bahnhof kommt?

Compare the following sentences:

Ich weiß den Weg.
Ich kenne den Weg.

The two sentences mean almost the same thing. Both would be translated as "I know the way" in English. In the first sentence, however, intellectual knowledge is stressed and it could be the case that the person has never gone that way before. In the second sentence, personal experience of already having been that way is stressed.

Kennen cannot be used in main clauses that have subordinate clauses.

The verbs kennen and wissen are irregular. You will find their forms in the list of irregular verbs. (→ 📖 **Appendix 3**)

3 The verb lassen

Lassen can have the following meanings:

to not take, ie to leave	Ich lasse das Auto zu Hause und fahre mit der Straßenbahn.
to permit	Wir lassen unsere Kinder nachts nicht in die Stadt.
someone else is doing sth	Er lässt sich die Haare schneiden.
to forbid	Lass das!
to not allow	Lass dich nicht ärgern.
to not do / to stop	Ich glaube, ich lasse das heute und arbeite lieber morgen weiter.

Lassen is irregular. You will find its various forms in the list of irregular verbs. (→ 📖 **Appendix 3**)

4 The verb werden

The verb werden can be used in the following ways:

main verb (change/ development)	Ich **werde** jetzt gleich wütend.
	Es **wird** Sommer.
	Peter **wird** Techniker.
	Das **wird** schon wieder.
	Es **wird** alles wieder gut.
auxiliary verb (passive) (→ 📖 **C 21**)	Peter **wird** zum Techniker **ausgebildet**.
	Das Haus **ist** in nur drei Wochen **gebaut worden**.
auxiliary verb (future) (→ 📖 **C 19.7**)	Ich **werde** dich nie **vergessen**.
	Wir **werden** ab morgen jeden Tag Sport **machen**.

Werden is irregular. You will find its various forms in the list of irregular verbs. (→ 📖 **Appendix 3, C 19.5**)

Nouns

The words in bold type in the text below are nouns.
In German, nouns always begin with a capital letter.

Verschiedenes **Bedürfen**[1]

Man erzählt, ein **Hund** und ein **Pferd** waren befreundet. Der **Hund** sparte[2] dem **Pferd** die besten **Knochen** auf und das **Pferd** legte dem **Hund** die duftigsten **Heubündel** vor und so wollte jeder dem anderen das **Liebste** tun und so wurde keiner von beiden satt.

Ernst Bloch (philosopher)

[1] verschiedenes Bedürfen = verschiedene Bedürfnisse
[2] aufsparen = etwas für jemanden aufbewahren

Three things about nouns are important:

Gender	The article der, das, die indicates the grammatical gender of a noun.
Number	Most nouns have a singular and a plural form: der Stuhl – die Stühle.
Case	Nouns can be declined: der Stuhl, auf dem Stuhl.

In German there are three genders:

Masculine: der	*Neuter:* das	*Feminine:* die
der Hund	das Pferd	die Kursleiterin
der Knochen	das Heu	die Teilnehmerliste
der Deutschkurs	das Deutschbuch	die Kassette
der Text	das Fahrrad	die Philosophie

Except for the "natural" gender of people, the gender of a noun can not be predicted.

The gender of a noun determines its declension. (→ 📖 C 34–37)
For this reason, you should always learn a noun together with its article.

There are large groups of nouns which are always neuter:

nominalized verbs	das Lieben, das Lernen, das Sprechen
nouns ending in -chen, -lein	das Häuschen, das Blümlein

Nouns with the following endings are always feminine:

-ung, -heit,	die Rechnung, die Freiheit,
-keit, -tät,	die Höflichkeit, die Universität,
-schaft, -tion,	die Freundschaft, die Nation,
-ei, -ur	die Metzgerei, die Natur

30 Compound nouns

The gender of a compound noun is determined by the final noun – the base word.

die Kursteilnehmerin der Kurs + die Teilnehmerin
der Zertifikatskurs das Zertifikat + der Kurs

(See also → 📖 C 7.6)

31 Number: singular and plural

Most nouns have both singular and plural forms.

Elefanten   Vögel   Tiger   Katzen

Fahrräder

Autos   Mäuse

Some nouns have

no plural: der Hunger, das Glück, das Obst, die Gesundheit, der Frieden
no singular: die Kosten, die Ferien, die Leute, die Eltern

32 Plural endings

By far the most common plural endings are -(e)n and -n.
Most masculine nouns have the ending -e in the plural.
The majority of feminine nouns end in -(e)n in the plural.

Below are the five most important plural endings. The stem vowel of some nouns in groups 1–3 also changes (a → ä, o → ö, u → ü).

1.	der Kilometer	die Kilometer	-	Nouns ending in -er, -en, -el, -chen, -lein do not have plural endings.
	der Vater	die Väter	¨-	
	die Mutter	die Mütter		

2.	der Kurs	die Kurse	-e	Most masculine, monosyllabic
	das Pferd	die Pferde		feminine and neuter nouns.
	die Nacht	die Nächte	¨-e	
	der Ball	die Bälle		

3.	das Kind	die Kinder	-er	Monosyllabic neuter and some
	der Mann	die Männer	¨-er	masculine nouns.
	das Wort	die Wörter		

4.	die Frau	die Frauen	-(e)n	Most feminine nouns and some
	die Lampe	die Lampen		masculine and neuter nouns, the
	der Student	die Studenten		n-class nouns. (→ 📖 C 35)
	die Lehrerin	die Lehrerinnen		▲ Feminine nouns with an -in ending need an additional -n before the plural ending.

| 5. | das Auto | die Autos | -s | Nouns ending in -a, -i, -o, -u, and |
| | der Test | die Tests | | many foreign words. (→ 📖 C 33) |

33 Plural endings of foreign words

Many foreign words have the plural ending -en.

das Gymnasium   die Gymnasien
das Datum   die Daten
das Museum   die Museen

Some foreign words retain their "foreign" endings.

das Lexikon   die Lexika
das Praktikum   die Praktika
das Visum   die Visa
der Index   die Indizes

In the following text, the word Mann appears in two different forms and the article in four forms.

Das ist ein Mann.
Der Mann ist groß und stark.
Man muss **den** Mann immer lieb haben.
Man muss **dem** Mann sagen, wie toll er ist.
Die Psyche **des** Mannes ist sehr sensibel.

There are four cases in German.
The determiners indicate the case.
(→ 📖 C 38–61)
In the singular, there are four declension forms for nouns:

	Masculine 1	Masculine 2 (n-class nouns)	Feminine	Neuter
Nominative	der Mann	der Junge	die Frau	das Haus
Accusative	den Mann	den Jungen	die Frau	das Haus
Dative	dem Mann	dem Jungen	der Frau	dem Haus
Genitive	des Mannes	des Jungen	der Frau	des Hauses

For monosyllabic nouns and nouns ending in -s, -ß, -x, -z, -tz, -ch, the genitive ending is -**es**: des Hauses, des Gesetzes, des Buches.
The genitive ending of proper names is -s: Brechts Gedichte, Karls Computer.

In the plural, nouns only have a case ending in the dative.
The dative plural case ending is always n.

Dative plural	den Männern	den Jungen	den Frauen	den Häusern

The dative -n is not added if a noun already ends with an -n or if a noun forms the plural with an -s: (→ 📖 C 32)

den Mädchen, den Ideen …
den Autos, den Kinos …

35   N-class nouns ("weak" masculine nouns)

Nouns do not have many different case endings in German (see C 34). You just have to learn the n-class nouns (or "weak" masculine nouns). The rest is easy.

The n-class nouns can be divided into three groups:

1 Masculine nouns ending with an -e (people, animals and some abstract nouns)	der Junge, der Kollege, der Pole, der Franzose, der Tiger, der Löwe …
Some masculine nouns ending with an -e add an -s in the genitive case	der Name – des Namens der Friede – des Friedens der Gedanke – des Gedankens …
2 Some other masculine nouns	der Mensch, der Bauer, der Herr …
3 Masculine nouns derived from Latin or Greek (ending with -and/-ant, -ent, -ist, -oge, -at)	der Doktorand, der Praktikant, der Patient, der Jurist, der Biologe, der Demokrat …

36 The function of case in sentences

C 94–97 explains how the verb structures the sentence in German. Nouns (as well as determiners and pronouns → ▢ C 38–61) can have different functions in a sentence. For example:

1 Nominative case (Question: Wer?)

Nominative/subject complements – All verbs require a subject complement.	**Frau Chaptal** wohnt in Seckenheim.
Some verbs have two nominative complements (eg bleiben, heißen, sein, werden).	**Ihr Mann** heißt **Bernard.**

2 Accusative case (Question: Wen?)

Many verbs require an accusative complement.	Buchstabieren Sie bitte **Ihren Namen.**
The objects of some prepositions are always in the accusative case. (→ ▢ C 79, 81)	– **Für wen** kaufst du **die Rosen?** + **Für meinen Mann.** – Wirklich?

Some prepositions require the accusative case in some instances (movement of an object in a particular direction) and the dative case in others (object remaining in one place). (→ ▢ C 81)

3 Dative case (Question: Wem?)

Certain verbs always require a dative complement.	Das Bild **gefällt meinem Vater** nicht. Das Bild **gehört meinem Bruder**.
Some prepositions always require the dative case. (→ 📖 **C 80**)	**Von den Häusern** da drüben bis **zum See** sind es nur 200 Meter.

4 Genitive case (Question: Wessen?)

There are only a few verbs that require genitive complements.	Mozarts Opern *(genitive)* die Opern Mozarts *(genitive)*
In spoken German, the genitive case is often replaced by the dative, together with the preposition von.	die Opern von Mozart *(dative)*

The genitive can, for example,

indicate "ownership"	Claudines Mann … Das Auto **meines Bruders** …
indicate authorship	Dürers Zeichnungen … Die Romane Thomas Manns …
combine a part with the whole	40 % **aller Österreicher** … Die Mehrheit **der Deutschen** …
The genitive case can also follow some prepositions. (→ 📖 **C 82**)	Trotz **des Regens** … Innerhalb **der Stadt** …

37 Nouns in dictionaries

You can identify the grammatical gender, plural form and declension of a noun in a dictionary:

gender genitive form*

Ti·ger [ti:ger] *m* ⟨-s; -⟩ *zo.* tiger ~fell *n* tiger skin

gender genitive form* plural

Tipp *der; -s, -s;* **1** ein nützlicher Rat, ein guter Hinweis ⟨von j-m e-n Tipp bekommen; j-m e-n Tipp geben⟩: *Tipps für den Anfänger, für den Garten* **2** der Versuch, bei Wetten und Ge-

*Not all dictionaries indicate the genitive form.

You should always learn a noun together with its article and plural form.

Determiners and pronouns

38   Determiners

The words in bold type in the dialogue are determiners.

– Kennst du **diesen** Mann?
+ **Welchen** Mann?
– Ich meine **den** Mann mit **dem** blauen Pullover.
+ Nein, **diesen** Mann kenne ich nicht. Aber vielleicht kennt ihn **meine** Freundin.

There are different types of determiners:

	Examples
Articles	der, das die, einer, ein, eine
Demonstratives	dieser, jener, der, das, die …
Indefinites	einige, viele, alle, jemand, niemand …
Possessives	mein, dein, sein …
Interrogatives	welcher, was für ein …

Determiners always have the same gender, number and case as the nouns which they precede:

– Siehst du **den Hund** dort?   Masculine, singular, accusative case
+ Das ist **mein Hund**.   Masculine, singular, nominative case

39   Pronouns

The words in bold type in the dialogue are pronouns.

– Kennst du **den** dort?
+ **Welchen**?
– **Den** mit dem blauen Pullover.
+ Nein, aber vielleicht kennt **ihn** meine Freundin. **Die** kennt fast **alle**.

Pronouns can replace or stand for nouns.
They can also replace entire clauses and sentences.

– Frau Buarque ist krank.   + Ja, ich habe **es** schon gehört.

There are various types of pronouns in German:

	Examples
Demonstrative pronouns	der, dieser, jener …
Indefinite pronouns	jemand, etwas, einer …
Interrogative pronouns	wer, was, welcher, was für einer …
Possessive pronouns	meiner, deiner, ihrer …
Personal pronouns	ich, du, er, es, sie …
Reflexive pronouns	mich, mir, dich, dir, sich …
Relative pronouns	der, das, die, welcher, was, wo …

The examples in **C 38** und **C 39** show that there are many words in German that can be both determiners and pronouns.

Determiner	*Pronoun*
– Kennst du **den** Mann?	+ Kennst du **den**?
+ **Welchen** Mann?	– **Welchen**?
– Na, **den** Mann da drüben.	+ Na, **den** da drüben.

Some words have different endings as determiners and pronouns:

– Hast du ein Taschentuch?	– Ist das mein Deutschbuch?
+ Ja, ich habe eins.	+ Nein, das ist meins.

40   Articles

Look at the pictures and read the sentences. The words in bold type are articles.

Das ist **ein** Hund.   **Der** Hund ist sehr groß.

There are: *definite articles*   der, das, die
           indefinite articles ein, eine

The indefinite article (ein, eine …) refers to something new.	Ich habe mir **ein** Fahrrad gekauft.
The definite article (der, das, die) refers to something known.	**Das** (Fahrrad) ist einfach super!

41 Declension of the definite article *der, das, die*

Singular	*Masculine*	*Neuter*	*Feminine*
Nominative	der Mann	das Kind	die Frau
Accusative	den Mann	das Kind	die Frau
Dative	dem Mann	dem Kind	der Frau
Genitive	des Mannes	des Kindes	der Frau

Plural	*Masculine*	*Neuter*	*Feminine*
Nominative	die Männer/Kinder/Frauen		
Accusative	die Männer/Kinder/Frauen		
Dative	den Männern/Kindern/Frauen		
Genitive	der Männer/Kinder/Frauen		

42 Declension of the indefinite article *ein, eine*

Singular	*Masculine*	*Neuter*	*Feminine*
Nominative	ein Mann	ein Kind	eine Frau
Accusative	einen Mann	ein Kind	eine Frau
Dative	einem Mann	einem Kind	einer Frau
Genitive	eines Mannes	eines Kindes	einer Frau

Plural	*Masculine*	*Neuter*	*Feminine*
Nominative	– Männer/Kinder/Frauen		
Accusative	– Männer/Kinder/Frauen		
Dative	– Männern/Kindern/Frauen		
Genitive	– Männern/Kindern/Frauen		

In German, there is no indefinite article in the plural.
When used as pronouns, ein/eine are declined like the definite article.
(→ 📖 C 41)

43 Demonstratives

The words in bold type in the following
dialogue are demonstratives.

– Welcher Rock gefällt Ihnen am
besten? **Dieser?**
+ Nein, **der** nicht. Ich hätte gern **den**
da drüben.
– Ja, **der** steht Ihnen wirklich gut.

Demonstratives are used to refer to things
or people in the vicinity, or to something
someone has said previously.
Demonstratives can be determiners and
pronouns. (→ 📖 C 44)

44 Declension of the demonstratives *dieser* and *jener*

Whether used as a determiner or a pronoun, dieser and jener are declined in the same
way. They are declined exactly like the definite article. (→ 📖 41)

Singular	Masculine	Neuter	Feminine
Nominative	dieser (Mann)	dieses (Kind)	diese (Frau)
Accusative	diesen (Mann)	dieses (Kind)	diese (Frau)
Dative	diesem (Mann)	diesem (Kind)	dieser (Frau)
Genitive	dieses Mannes	dieses Kindes	dieser Frau

Plural	Masculine	Neuter	Feminine
Nominative	diese (Männer/Kinder/Frauen)		
Accusative	diese (Männer/Kinder/Frauen)		
Dative	diesen (Männern/Kindern/Frauen)		
Genitive	dieser (Männer/Kinder/Frauen)		

45 Declension of the demonstratives *der, das, die*

As pronouns, der, das, die are declined almost like the definite article.
The exceptions are printed in bold type in the table.

Singular	Masculine	Neuter	Feminine
Nominative	der	das	die
Accusative	den	das	die
Dative	dem	dem	der
Genitive	**dessen**	**dessen**	**deren/derer**

Plural	Masculine	Neuter	Feminine
Nominative	die		
Accusative	die		
Dative	**denen**		
Genitive	**deren/derer**		

The genitive forms are rarely used. You need not learn them.

46 Indefinites

The words in bold type are indefinites.

In unserem Kurs treiben fast **alle** Sport. **Viele** fahren Ski. **Einige** gehen wandern und **jemand** macht sogar Triathlon. Aber **niemand** spielt Fußball. Nur Tom treibt **keinen** Sport. Der macht am liebsten **nichts** oder er geht höchstens mal **etwas** spazieren.

Indefinites indicate a quantity which is not clearly defined.

47 *nichts, etwas*

Ich sehe **nichts**. Mach mal Licht.

Jetzt sehe ich **etwas**.

The pronouns nichts and etwas are used only to refer to things.
They always have the same form.

48 *niemand, jemand, man*

– Kann mir **jemand** sagen, wie viele Einwohner die Stadt Lagos hat?
+ Ich glaube, das weiß **niemand** so genau.
– Na ja, **man** kann ja nicht alles wissen.

The pronouns jemand, niemand, man are only used to refer to people.
They can always be used in the same form.
Jemand and niemand are sometimes declined.

Man can be used to make general statements, or when you don't want to say, or don't know, who is responsible for an action.
(→ 📖 C 21)

Man darf hier nicht rauchen.
In Deutschland isst **man** zum Frühstück manchmal ein Ei.
Man hat mir mein Fahrrad gestohlen.

Man usually refers to several people, but the verb is always in the 3rd person singular.

49 *kein*

As a determiner, kein has the same forms as ein. (→ 📖 C 42)
Kein (unlike ein) also has plural forms.

Singular	Masculine	Neuter	Feminine
Nominative	kein Mann	kein Kind	keine Frau
Accusative	keinen Mann	kein Kind	keine Frau
Dative	keinem Mann	keinem Kind	keiner Frau
Genitive	keines Mannes	keines Kindes	keiner Frau

Plural	Masculine	Neuter	Feminine
Nominative	keine Männer/Kinder/Frauen		
Accusative	keine Männer/Kinder/Frauen		
Dative	keinen Männern/Kindern/Frauen		
Genitive	keiner Männer/Kinder/Frauen		

The genitive forms are rarely used. You need not learn them.

As a pronoun, keiner is declined like the definite article. (→ 📖 **C 41**)

Singular	Masculine	Neuter	Feminine
Nominative	keiner	keins	keine
Accusative	keinen	keins	keine
Dative	keinem	keinem	keiner
Genitive	keines	keines	keiner

Plural	Masculine	Neuter	Feminine
Nominative	keine		
Accusative	keine		
Dative	keinen		
Genitive	keiner		

50 *mancher, manches, manche*

− **Manche** Deutsche essen gerne Schweinebraten.
+ Ja, aber **manchen** ist Schweinebraten viel zu fett.

The declension is as for kein. (→ 📖 **C 49**)

51 Interrogatives

− **Wer** ist der neue Freund von Norma?
+ Der dort drüben.
− **Welchen** meinst du.
+ Den mit dem Jackett.
− Da sind zwei mit Jackett. **Was für eine** Farbe hat es?
+ Grau.
− Ach der! Den kenne ich doch.

Interrogatives are question words which accompany or replace nouns. They are used to ask about both people and things.

Interrogatives are used in direct questions and in indirect questions.

− **Wer** kann mich nach Hause fahren?
+ Ich, aber ich weiß nicht, **wo** du wohnst.

Interrogatives (overview)..	Asking about ....
– Wer fährt mich nach Hause?	person nominative
+ Peter.	
– Wen hast du schon gefragt?	accusative
+ Frau Klein.	
– Wem hast du mein Buch gegeben?	dative
+ Einer Kollegin.	
– Wessen Kuli ist das hier?	genitive
+ Meiner.	
– Was hast du gestern gemacht?	action or thing
+ Nichts.	
– Wo wohnst du?	place
+ In der Willy-Brandt-Straße 12.	
– Woher kommen Sie?	origin/direction
+ Aus Gotha.	
– Wohin geht ihr?	destination/direction
+ Nach Hause.	
– Wann kommst du nach Hause?	time
+ Um 12.	
– Wie lange arbeitest du noch?	duration
+ Eine Stunde.	
– Warum hast du mich nicht angerufen?	reason
+ Mein Handy ist kaputt.	
– Wie heißen Sie?	composition, state, manner
+ Kobelmüller	
– Wie schreibt man das?	
– Wie viele Leute sind in deinem Kurs?	countable quantity
+ 15.	
– Wie viel Zeit brauchst du zum Lernen?	non-countable quantity
+ Etwa eine Stunde täglich.	
– Welches Kleid soll ich heute anziehen?	selection from a specific
+ Zieh doch das blaue an.	quantity
– Was für ein Kleid soll ich heute anziehen?	selection: style type
+ Ein sommerliches. Es ist warm heute.	
– Was für ein Kleid hast du gekauft?	declension like ein, eine
+ Ein leichtes für den Sommer.	as a determiner or ...
– Ich habe einen neuen Computer.	
+ Oh, toll, was für einer ist es?	... pronoun (→ 📖 **C 42**)

52 *welcher, welches, welche*

Whether used as a determiner or a pronoun, they are declined like the definite article.
(→ 📖 C 41)

Singular	*Masculine*	*Neuter*	*Feminine*
Nominative	welcher (Mann)?	welches (Kind)?	welche (Frau)?
Accusative	welchen (Mann)?	welches (Kind)?	welche (Frau)?
Dative	welchem (Mann)?	welchem (Kind)?	welcher (Frau)?
Genitive	welchen Mannes?	welchen Kindes?	welcher Frau?

Plural	*Masculine*	*Neuter*	*Feminine*
Nominative	welche (Männer/Kinder/Frauen)?		
Accusative	welche (Männer/Kinder/Frauen)?		
Dative	welchen (Männern/Kindern/Frauen)?		
Genitive	welcher Männer/Kinder/Frauen?		

53 Personal pronouns

Personal pronouns can

represent people involved in a conversation:

– Kannst **du mir** bitte mein Kursbuch geben?
+ **Ich** weiß doch nicht, wo dein Kursbuch ist.

refer to people or things mentioned previously:

Klaus Meier kommt aus Eisenach. **Er** arbeitet bei Opel. Seine Freundin heißt

Petra. **Er** liebt **sie** sehr und **sie ihn** auch. Im Juli hat Petra Geburtstag. Klaus
schenkt **ihr** ein neues Fahrrad.

In formal address, personal pronouns begin with a capital letter.

Sehr geehrte Frau Self,

ich darf Ihnen herzlich im Namen unserer Firma zu Ihrem Geburtstag gratulieren. Wir hoffen, dass Sie Ihren Festtag im Kreis Ihrer Familie genießen können, und freuen uns auf die weitere Zusammenarbeit mit Ihnen.

Mit freundlichen Grüßen

Ludwig Lollmann
(Personalchef)

Personal pronouns are rarely used in the genitive case.

		Nominative	*Accusative*	*Dative*	*Genitive*
Singular	*1st person*	ich	mich	mir	meiner
	2nd person	du	dich	dir	deiner
	3rd person	er	ihn	ihm	seiner
		es	es	ihm	seiner
		sie	sie	ihr	ihrer
Plural	*1st person*	wir	uns	uns	uns(e)rer*
	2nd person	ihr	euch	euch	eu(e)rer*
	3rd person	sie	sie	ihnen	ihrer
Formal address		Sie	Sie	Ihnen	Ihrer

*The e before the r is usually dropped.

The words in bold type are possessives. Possessives indicate ownership or affiliation.

Schauen Sie, hier in der Mitte, das ist **unser** Sohn Mark. Rechts von **ihm** steht **seine** Frau Susi und vorne sitzen **ihre** Kinder: Daniel, Petra und Karin. Sie stehen vor **ihrem** Haus. Daniel hat sogar **sein** eigenes Zimmer. Das da oben rechts ist **seins**.

Possessives can be determiners or pronouns.

– Ist das **Ihre** Katze?
+ Nein, **meine** frisst keine Vögel.
– Und wo ist **Ihre**?
+ **Meine** Katze ist zu Hause.

In formal address, possessives always begin with a capital letter.

The forms of pos- sessive determiners and pronouns:	*Personal pron.* *Nominative*	*Possessive determ.* *Nominative*	*Possessive pron.* *Nominative*
	ich	mein Buch	meins
	du	dein Buch	deins
	er	sein Buch	seins
	sie	ihr Buch	ihrs
	es	sein Buch	seins
	wir	unser Buch	uns(e)res*
*The e before the r	ihr	euer Buch	eu(e)res*
is usually dropped.	sie	ihr Buch	ihres

Possessive determiners are declined like the determiner kein. (→ 📖 C 49)
All possessives have the same endings.

Singular	*Masculine*	*Neuter*	*Feminine*
Nominative	mein Hund	mein Auto	meine Banane
Accusative	meinen Hund	mein Auto	meine Banane
Dative	meinem Hund	meinem Auto	meiner Banane
Genitive	meines Hundes	meines Autos	meiner Banane

Plural	*Masculine*	*Neuter*	*Feminine*
Nominative	meine Hunde/Autos/Bananen		
Accusative	meine Hunde/Autos/Bananen		
Dative	meinen Hunden/Autos/Bananen		
Genitive	meiner Hunde/Autos/Bananen		

Possessive pronouns are declined like the pronoun kein. (→ 📖 C 49)

Singular	*Masculine*	*Neuter*	*Feminine*
Nominative	meiner	meins	meine
Accusative	meinen	meins	meine
Dative	meinem	meinem	meiner
Genitive	meines	meine	meiner

Plural	*Masculine*	*Neuter*	*Feminine*
Nominative	meine		
Accusative	meine		
Dative	meinen		
Genitive	meiner		

57 Reflexive pronouns

Certain verbs require reflexive pronouns. (→ 📖 C 26)
A reflexive pronoun takes the accusative or dative case, depending on the verb.

	Reflexive pronouns in the accusative		*Reflexive pronouns in the dative*	
1st person singular	Ich ärgere	mich.	Ich gefalle	mir.
2nd person singular	Du ärgerst	dich.	Du gefällst	dir.
3rd person singular	Er/Es/Sie ärgert	**sich.**	Er/Es/Sie gefällt	**sich.**
1st person plural	Wir ärgern	uns.	Wir gefallen	uns.
2nd person plural	Ihr ärgert	euch.	Ihr gefallt	euch.
3rd person plural	Sie ärgern	**sich.**	Sie gefallen	**sich.**
Formal address	Sie ärgern	**sich.**	Sie gefallen	**sich.**

Most forms are identical with the personal pronouns in the accusative and dative cases.
The only exceptions are the 3rd person singular and plural: sich. (→ 📖 C 54, C 26)

58 Relative pronouns

Eine Maschine, **die** Wäsche wäscht, heißt auf Deutsch Waschmaschine.

Da drüben geht der Mann, **den** ich gestern auf dem Bahnhof gesehen habe.

Relative pronouns refer to something that has already been mentioned.
They introduce relative clauses. (→ 📖 C 101.4)

The gender and number of the relative pronoun depends upon the word it refers to:

Die Firma, für **die** ich zehn Jahre gearbeitet habe, hat mich entlassen.
└→ *feminine singular*

The case which the relative pronoun takes depends upon the verb or preposition:

Die Firma, **bei der** ich zehn Jahre   bei + *dative*
gearbeitet habe, hat mich entlassen.

Die Firma, **der** ich meine Karriere   verdanken + *dative*
verdanke, gibt es leider nicht mehr.

GRAMMAR ⋮ 168

Der, das, die as relative pronouns are declined like der, das, die as demonstrative pronouns. (→ 📖 C 45)

Singular .... Masculine.........

Nominative	Der Film, **der** jetzt im Kino läuft, ist super!
Accusative	Der Film, **den** ich gestern gesehen habe, ist langweilig.
Dative	Der Film, von **dem** ich dir erzählt habe, läuft nicht mehr.
Genitive	Der Film, **dessen** Anfang so traurig ist, hat ein Happy End.

Singular .... Neuter.........

Nominative	Das Buch, **das** auf Platz 1 der Bestsellerliste ist, ist super!
Accusative	Das Buch, **das** ich gestern gelesen habe, ist langweilig.
Dative	Das Buch, von **dem** ich dir erzählt habe, ist nicht mehr da.
Genitive	Das Buch, **dessen** Anfang so traurig ist, hat ein Happy End.

Singular .... Feminine.........

Nominative	Die Geschichte, **die** in der Zeitung steht, ist super!
Accusative	Die Geschichte, **die** ich gestern gehört habe, ist langweilig.
Dative	Die Geschichte, von **der** ich dir erzählt habe, ist nicht wahr.
Genitive	Die Geschichte, **deren** Anfang so traurig ist, hat ein Happy End.

Plural .... Masculine/Neuter/Feminine.........

Nominative	Die Bücher, **die** auf der Bestsellerliste sind, sind super.
Accusative	Die Bücher, **die** ich letzte Woche gelesen habe, sind langweilig.
Dative	Die Bücher, von **denen** ich dir erzählt habe, sind nicht mehr da.
Genitive	Die Bücher, **deren** Anfang traurig ist, haben oft ein Happy End.

60 **Other relative pronouns**

60.1 *welcher, welches, welche*

Welcher, welches, welche are sometimes used in written German for stylistic reasons. They replace the relative pronouns der, das or die.

Der Schaden, **welcher** der Firma entstanden ist, wird von der Versicherung bezahlt.	instead of: Der Schaden, **der** der Firma entstanden ist …

As relative pronouns, welcher, welches and welche are declined exactly like they are as interrogatives. (→ 📖 C 52)

60.2 *was*

Was is used after

Superlatives:	Das ist das Schönste, **was** ich je gesehen habe.
Ordinal numbers:	Das Erste, **was** er von Wien sah, war der Stephansdom.
Indefinites:	Alles, **was** du sagst, ist richtig.
alles, vieles, einiges,	Einiges, **was** er getan hat, verstehe ich nicht.
manches, weniges,	Es gibt etwas, **was** ich dir sagen muss.
etwas, nichts	Sprich bitte lauter. Ich verstehe nichts!
das	Das, **was** du sagst, ist richtig.

61 *es*

In German sentences, the word es is a "building block" which often has no meaning of its own, but which is needed for syntactic reasons.
The word es has three different functions:

1 Pronoun:

– Wo ist mein **Buch**?
+ **Es** liegt neben dir auf dem Stuhl.

2 Formal or "dummy" subject (nominative complement), when a sentence has no other subject:

Es regnet, es schneit, es ist kalt, hoffentlich kommt bald besseres Wetter.
Es gibt kein schlechtes Wetter. Es gibt nur schlechte Kleidung.
Es geht mir gut.
Es ist verboten, im Bus zu rauchen.
Es ist möglich, dass er morgen nach Hause kommt.
Es tut mir Leid, wenn ich dir wehgetan habe.

3 "Fill-in" in the 1st position before the verb:

1	2	
Es	wird	eine Woche lang gefeiert.

It can be omitted if the sentence is reformulated:

Eine Woche lang	wird	gefeiert.

Adjectives

62   Introduction

The American author Mark Twain wrote:
„Wenn dem Deutschen ein Adjektiv in die Finger fällt, dekliniert und dekliniert und dekliniert er es, bis aller gesunde Menschenverstand herausdekliniert ist. [...] Ich habe einen Studenten in einem seiner ruhigsten Augenblicke einmal sagen hören, lieber beuge ich hundertmal beide Knie als auch nur eine einziges Adjektiv, und es handelte sich nicht etwa um einen Turner."
(In: Herbert Genzmer, Deutsche Grammatik, Insel Verlag, Frankfurt am Main, 1995, p. 219)

63   What are adjectives?

The words in bold type in the following text are adjectives.

Asterix ist **klug**. Er läuft sehr **schnell**. Der **dicke** Obelix ist sein **bester** Freund. Obelix hat einen **kleinen** Hund: Idefix. Obelix hat immer **großen** Hunger. Er findet besonders Wildschweine sehr **gut**. Obelix ist sehr **stark**. Er ist der **stärkste** Mann im Dorf.

With adjectives you can

describe someone or something:	Asterix ist klug.
say how someone does something: (In German, most adjectives can be used as adverbs.)	Asterix läuft schnell.
make comparisons:	Obelix ist stärker als Asterix. Er ist der stärkste Mann im Dorf.

Adjectives change their form.

They can be declined: (→ 📖 C 67–69)	Asterix hat einen starken Freund. Ein dicker Bauch, ein freundliches Gesicht, das ist Obelix.
... and they have comparative and superlative forms: (→ 📖 C 70–71)	stark – stärker – am stärksten gut – besser – am besten schnell – schneller – am schnellsten

64 Adjectives after nouns

<u>Fabiane</u> ist **intelligent** und **fleißig**.
<u>Sie</u> arbeitet **schnell** und **effizient**.
<u>Tom</u> ist **freundlich** und **kontaktfreudig**.
<u>Die Fabrik</u> von Opel in Eisenach arbeitet fast **vollautomatisch**.

If an adjective comes after the noun or pronoun which it refers to, it is not declined.

65 Adjectives before nouns

Die Unternehmen wollen heute nur noch den flexiblen, teamfähigen Mitarbeiter / die flexible, teamfähige Mitarbeiterin mit hervorragend**em** Schulabschluss. Er oder sie soll am besten über eine solide Berufausbildung verfügen und 10 Jahre Berufserfahrung haben. Er oder sie sollte aber nicht älter als dreißig sein.

An adjective which comes before a noun is declined. Its ending depends upon the gender, case and number of the noun it modifies.

Der **schöne** Mann weint. Er hat seine **intelligente** Freundin verloren.

Gender: masculine	*Gender: feminine*
Case: nominative (Wer?)	*Case: accusative* (Wen?)
Number: singular	*Number: singular*

66 Declension of adjectives

There are three declension types.

1. following the definite article (der, das, die)   der flexible Mitarbeiter
2. following the indefinite article (ein, eine)   ein flexibler Mitarbeiter
3. placed alone before a noun   flexibler Mitarbeiter

There are also other words (for example indefinites) after which adjectives are declined either as type 1 or as type 2. (→ 📖 C 67–68)

67 Adjectival declension: type 1

Adjectives that come after the definite article (der, das, die) can have two different endings:

Singular	Masculine	Neuter	Feminine
Nominative	der rote Hut	das rote Auto	die rote Hose
Accusative	den roten Hut	das rote Auto	die rote Hose
Dative	dem roten Hut	dem roten Auto	der roten Hose
Genitive	des roten Hutes	des roten Autos	der roten Hose

Plural	Masculine	Neuter	Feminine
Nominative	die roten Hüte/Autos/Hosen		
Accusative	die roten Hüte/Autos/Hosen		
Dative	den roten Hüten/Autos/Hosen		
Genitive	der roten Hüte/Autos/Hosen		

Adjectives also take the above endings after: dieser, jeder, jener, mancher, welcher.

68 Adjectival declension: type 2

Adjectives that come after indefinite article (ein, eine) and kein, keine have the following endings:

Singular	Masculine	Neuter	Feminine
Nominative	kein roter Hut	kein rotes Auto	keine rote Hose
Accusative	keinen roten Hut	kein rotes Auto	keine rote Hose
Dative	keinem roten Hut	keinem roten Auto	keiner roten Hose
Genitive	keines roten Hutes	keines roten Autos	keiner roten Hose

Plural	Masculine	Neuter	Feminine
Nominative	keine roten Hüte/Autos/Hosen		
Accusative	keine roten Hüte/Autos/Hosen		
Dative	keinen roten Hüten/Autos/Hosen		
Genitive	keiner roten Hüte/Autos/Hosen		

In German, there is no indefinite article in the plural.

Adjectives that come after possessives (mein, dein, sein, ihr, unser, euer, ihr) also take the above endings.

If an adjective comes before a noun that has no article, its last letter is the same as the last letter of the corresponding definite article (exceptions: genitive masc. + neut. sing.).

der grüne Salat	grüner Salat
das frische Gemüse	frisches Gemüse
die weiße Schokolade	weiße Schokolade
die blauen Trauben	blaue Trauben

Singular	*Masculine*	*Neuter*	*Feminine*
Nominative	grüner Salat	frisches Gemüse	weiße Schokolade
Accusative	grünen Salat	frisches Gemüse	weiße Schokolade
Dative	grünem Salat	frischem Gemüse	weißer Schokolade
Genitive	grün<u>en</u> Salats	frisch<u>en</u> Gemüses	weißer Schokolade

Plural	*Masculine*	*Neuter*	*Feminine*
Nominative	blaue Trauben		
Accusative	blaue Trauben		
Dative	blauen Trauben		
Genitive	blauer Trauben		

Adjectives that come after some determiners and quantifiers without endings (einige, mehrere, etwas, mehr, zwei, drei …) are declined as above:

Für den Salat nehme ich etwas frischen Knoblauch, mehrere kleine Zwiebeln und fünf große Tomaten.

There are two forms of comparison.

Ein Spatz fliegt schnell.

Ein Kolibri fliegt viel schneller.

Am schnellsten fliegt der Stachelschwanzsegler (bis zu 171 km/h). Er ist der schnellste Vogel der Welt.

Most adjectives form the comparative and superlative in the following manner:

Basic form		schnell
Comparative	+ er	schnell**er**
Superlative	+ ste(n)	am schnell**sten** / der, das, die schnell**ste** …

An adjective in its comparative or superlative form is also declined if it comes before a noun. It then takes the same ending as it would in its original form.
(→ 📖 C 65–69)

Das frischeste Gemüse mit dem besten Geschmack kauft man beim Bauern.
Männer tragen heute modischere Kleidung als noch vor zehn Jahren.

71 Comparison of adjectives with an "umlaut" / irregular forms

The following adjectives change their vowels in the comparative and superlative forms:			
	alt	älter	am ältesten
	arg	ärger	am ärgsten
	arm	ärmer	am ärmsten
	dumm	dümmer	am dümmsten
	grob	gröber	am gröbsten
	groß	größer	am größten
	hart	härter	am härtesten
	jung	jünger	am jüngsten
	kalt	kälter	am kältesten
	klug	klüger	am klügsten
	krank	kränker	am kränksten
	kurz	kürzer	am kürzesten
	lang	länger	am längsten
	rot	röter	am rötesten
	scharf	schärfer	am schärfsten
	schwach	schwächer	am schwächsten
	schwarz	schwärzer	am schwärzesten
	stark	stärker	am stärksten
	warm	wärmer	am wärmsten

These adjectives have irregular forms in the comparative and super-lative:			
	gut	besser	am besten
	hoch	höher	am höchsten
	nah	näher	am nächsten
	viel	mehr	am meisten

72   Spelling of certain adjectives

In the comparative form, some adjectives drop an e for pronunciation reasons.

dunkel – dunkler   sauer – saurer   teuer – teurer

In the superlative form, some adjectives add an e for pronunciation reasons.

laut – lauter – am lautesten / der, das, die lauteste …

Numerals

73   Introduction

The most important kinds of numerals in German are:

Cardinal numbers (→ 📖 Appendix 1.1)	ein(s), zwei, dreizehn, vierundzwanzig, einhundertundfünf
Ordinal numbers (→ 📖 Appendix 1.1)	der/das/die erste, zweite, dreizehnte, vierundzwanzigste, einhundertfünfte
Fractions (→ 📖 Appendix 1.2)	halb, drittel, zehntel, hundertstel
Multiples	zweifach, doppelt, dreifach, zehnfach, hundertfach …

Some numerals are adverbs (→ 📖 C 90–92):

erstens, zweitens, drittens …	– Kannst du mir bei den Aufgaben helfen? + Nein, erstens habe ich keine Zeit und zweitens kannst du das allein.
einmal, zweimal, dreimal …	– Wer hat angerufen? + Dreimal darfst du raten.

74   Cardinal numbers

– Ich habe **drei** Kinder, **eine** Tochter und **zwei** Söhne. Wie viele Kinder haben Sie?
+ **Eins**. Eine Tochter.

Cardinal numbers are not declined.

⚠ The numeral eins never comes before a noun. Instead, the indefinite article (ein, eine) comes before a noun.

List of cardinal numbers → 📖 **Appendix 1.1**

```
┌──────┐
│  69
└──────┘
     ↓   ↓
```

⚠ Numbers from 13 to 99 are read from right to left.   neunundsechzig

75 Years

Years until 1099 and from 2000 are read like cardinal numbers.

800   Im Jahr achthundert wurde Karl der Große zum Kaiser gekrönt.
1066 (Ein)tausend(und)sechsundsechzig eroberte Wilhelm der Eroberer die Britischen Inseln.

Years from 1100 until 1999 are read as follows:

1886 18hundert86 erfand Gottlieb Daimler das Auto.
1957 Im Jahr 19hundert57 wurde die EWG, die europäische Wirtschaftsgemeinschaft, gegründet.

76 Ordinal numbers

Ordinal numbers are formed by adding suffixes:

1st –19th (1. - 19.)   *cardinal number* + te
20th (20.)   *cardinal number* + ste

There are a few exceptions. They are in bold type in the list in **Appendix 1.1**

With ordinal numbers you can

express sequence: Sie hat drei Töchter. Die **erste** heißt Selda, die **zweite** Laura und die **dritte** Julia.

give proportions: Jeder **dritte** Deutsche hält „Rechtsanwalt" für einen angesehenen Beruf und jeder **vierte** Deutsche „Fabrikdirektor".

indicate dates: Am **elften Elften** beginnt die Fastnachtszeit.

Ordinal numbers in names: Elisabeth I.   Elisabeth die Erste
                             Karl V.   Karl der Fünfte

Prepositions

The words in bold type in the following dialogue are prepositions.

– Entschuldigung, können Sie mir bitte sagen,
 wie ich am schnellsten **zum** Rathaus komme?
 Ich habe dort **um** zwei Uhr einen Termin.
+ Gehen Sie hier **über** den Platz und dann **in** die
 Hauptstraße. Die Hauptstraße **entlang** bis zur
 Heiliggeistkirche **am** Marktplatz. Der Eingang
 zum Rathaus ist **auf** der Ostseite **vom** Platz.
– Wie lange braucht man **bis** dahin?
+ Fünfzehn Minuten **zu** Fuß
– Und **mit** dem Auto?
+ Viel länger, weil Sie keinen Parkplatz finden.

Prepositions can have different meanings and functions.
Here are some examples:

referring to place (Wo?)	am Marktplatz, an der Wand, im Rathaus
referring to direction (Wohin?)	über den Bismarckplatz, in die Hauptstraße nach Italien, ins Tal
referring to time (Wann?)	um zwei Uhr, nach Mitternacht, im Winter, seit zwei Jahren
other meanings	mit dem Auto, zu Fuß, vom Marktplatz, auf Deutsch, aus Wolle, ohne Zucker

Prepositions are also often connected to certain verbs. They then no longer have their
own meaning. (→ 📖 C 83)

78   Links between articles and prepositions

For pronunciation reasons, the	am = an dem	ins = in das
article is often contracted and	beim = bei dem	zum = zu dem
joined to the preposition.	im = in dem	zur = zu der

– Was hast du **am** Samstag gemacht?
+ Morgens bin ich **im** Wald joggen gewesen und danach auf den Markt **zum**
 Einkaufen. Dann hab ich **beim** Italiener Mittag gegessen.

79 Prepositions taking the accusative

bis, durch, entlang, für, gegen, ohne, um, um … herum

Wir warten auf Ihre Antwort **bis** Dienstag, den 22. April.
Wir brauchen **für** den Vertrag noch Ihre Unterschrift.
Durch den harten Winter sind viele Bauarbeiter arbeitslos.
Die Regierung tut nichts **gegen** die Arbeitslosigkeit.
Ohne staatliche Maßnahmen kann man Arbeitslosigkeit nicht bekämpfen.
Was, es ist 10 Uhr und noch hell? **Um** diese Zeit ist es bei uns schon dunkel.
Gehen Sie **um** das Haus **herum**. Der Eingang ist auf der Rückseite.
Wenn Sie diese Straße **entlang**gehen, kommen Sie zum Bahnhof.

For further examples of the usage of these prepositions:
→ 📖 B 20.

80 Prepositions taking the dative

This mnemonic rhyme contains the seven most important dative prepositions:

The following also require the dative:
an … vorbei, außer, gegenüber

Von **Ausbeimit** nach **Vonseitzu**
fährst immer mit dem Dativ du.

Gehen Sie **an** der Kirche **vorbei**.
Sedat kommt **aus** der Türkei.
Außer einem Glas Wein habe ich nichts getrunken.
Aber **bei** der Polizeikontrolle habe ich doch Angst gehabt.
Das Rathaus steht **gegenüber** der Heiliggeistkirche.
Mit dem Fahrrad ist man in der Stadt heute meistens am schnellsten.
Nach dem Kino können wir ja noch was trinken gehen.
Der Film läuft erst **seit** einer Woche.
Ich habe eine Kinokarte **von** meinem Kollegen geschenkt bekommen.
Vom Marktplatz aus kann man das Heidelberger Schloss sehen.
Am Sonntag fahre ich **zu** meinen Eltern.

For further examples of the usage of the most important dative prepositions:
→ 📖 B 21.

81 Prepositions taking either the dative or the accusative

Certain prepositions sometimes take the dative and sometimes the accusative. The most important ones are: an, auf, hinter, in, neben, über, unter, vor, zwischen.

Peter und Ute gehen ins (in das) Kino.

Movement in a particular direction:
preposition + accusative

Peter und Ute sind im Kino.

Remaining in one place:
preposition + dative

Er hängt das Bild **an die** Wand.
Ich lege das Buch **auf deinen** Tisch.
Mario ist **hinter das** Haus gelaufen.
Setzten Sie sich doch links **neben mich**.
Das Schiff fährt **über den** See.
Stell das Fahrrad bitte **vor die** Tür.
Darf ich mich **zwischen euch** setzen?
(→ 📖 B 21)

Das Bild hängt **an der** Wand.
Das Buch liegt **auf deinem** Tisch.
Er spielt **hinter dem** Haus.
Rechts **neben mir** sitzt Frau Kohl.
Über dem See sieht man Wolken.
Es steht doch schon **vor der** Tür.
Ich sitze so gern **zwischen euch**.

82 Prepositions taking either the genitive or dative

These prepositions take either the genitive or the dative:

trotz, während,

wegen

Trotz des Regens haben wir unsere Wanderung gemacht.
Trotz dem Regen …

Während des Konzerts darf nicht fotografiert werden.
Während dem Konzert …

Wegen des Regens können wir nicht ins Schwimmbad.
Wegen dem Regen …

In these examples, the genitive is thought to be more refined, but is also considered "overly correct". The genitive is being used less and less nowadays.

The following prepositions always take the genitive:
außerhalb, innerhalb, oberhalb, unterhalb

Außerhalb der Stadt darf man in Deutschland 100 km/h schnell fahren.
Innerhalb der Stadt darf man nur 50 km/h fahren; in Wohngebieten 30 km/h.

(→ 📖 B 21)

83   Verbs with prepositions

Some verbs are linked to certain prepositions. In this case, these prepositions do not have a meaning of their own, but they change the meaning of the verb.

sich freuen auf   Ich freue mich auf das Wochenende.
sich freuen über   Egon freut sich über die Blumen.

reden von   Egon redet nur von seinen Kindern.
reden über   Wir müssen über das Problem reden.

You have to learn the verbs with prepositions. There is a list with the most important ones in the appendix: → 📖 **Appendix 2**.

Conjunctions

84   Introduction

Conjunctions link parts of sentences or texts.

Egon ist lieb **und** freundlich. Alle Frauen finden ihn toll, **weil** er so gut bügelt. Er kocht gern **und** (er) wäscht auch gern ab. Ich möchte ihm so gern sagen, **dass** ich ihn mag, **und** mit ihm ausgehen. Egon ist **weder** ein Macho **noch** ein Softie.

Conjunctions link

words and word groups:	**nett** und **freundlich**
sentences:	**Er kocht gern** und **er wäscht gern ab.**
main + subordinate clauses:	**Alle Frauen finden ihn toll,** weil **er so gut bügelt.**

85   Conjunctions which link words and word groups

(entweder ...) oder	Egon liest entweder ein Buch oder einen Comic.
nicht ..., sondern	Er arbeitet nicht in einer Firma, sondern zu Hause.
sowohl ... als auch	Er kann sowohl bügeln als auch kochen.
und	Er schreibt Gedichte und Geschichten.
weder ... noch	Egon hat weder Frau noch Kinder.
zwar ..., aber	Er lebt zwar allein, aber er hat viele Freunde.

86   Conjunctions which link sentences (coordinating conjunctions)

Sentence 1   *Sentence 2*

Egon (kocht) gern.   Er (wäscht) auch gern |ab).

Sentence 1   *Sentence 2*

Egon (kocht) gern   und   er (wäscht) auch gern |ab).

If two sentences (ie two main clauses) are linked with one of the following conjunctions, the word order in both clauses remains unchanged:

Reason	denn	Ich mag Egon, denn er ist wirklich sympathisch.
Contradiction	nicht ..., sondern	Er redet nicht viel, sondern (er) macht seine Arbeit.
Alternative	(entweder ...) oder	Abends liest er (entweder) ein Buch oder (er) sieht fern.
Concession	(zwar ...) aber	Egon ist (zwar) etwas schüchtern, aber er kann sehr charmant sein.

If the nominative complement (the subject) is the same in both clauses, it is often omitted in the second clause.

Er redet nicht viel, sondern (**er**) macht seine Arbeit.

Sentence 1

Alle Frauen (lieben) Egon.

Sentence 2

Egon (kann) gut (bügeln).

Main clause	*Conjunction*	*Subordinate clause*
Alle Frauen (lieben) Egon,	weil	er so gut (bügeln) (kann).

If two sentences are linked by a conjunction like weil (a subordinating conjunction), the word order in the subordinate clause (the sentence after weil) changes. The conjugated verb moves to the end of the sentence.
(→ 📖 C 101)

Here are some examples of subordinating conjunctions:

als	Ich war gerade zu Hause, als der Regen anfing.
als ob	Er sah aus, als ob er drei Tage nicht geschlafen hätte.
bevor	Ich zeigte ihm den Brief, bevor er etwas sagen konnte.
bis	Wir haben dann geredet, bis er einschlief.
da	Da ich heute krank bin, werde ich nicht ins Büro gehen.
damit	Ich bleibe im Bett, damit ich mich etwas ausruhe.
dass	Der Arzt sagt, dass ich weniger arbeiten soll.
ehe	Ich muss ganz gesund sein, ehe ich wieder arbeiten kann.
falls	Ruf mich an, falls etwas Wichtiges in der Firma passiert.
nachdem	Nachdem ich ausgeschlafen hatte, ging ich etwas spazieren.
ob	Ich weiß nicht, ob ich morgen schon wieder arbeiten kann.
obwohl	Ich fühle mich müde, obwohl ich lange geschlafen habe.
während	Während ich hier zu Hause bin, geht in der Firma sicher alles durcheinander.
seit	Es geht mir schon wieder besser, seit ich beim Arzt war.
weil	Ich muss bald wieder arbeiten, weil ich sonst mit meiner Arbeit nicht mehr zurechtkomme.
wenn (... dann)	Wenn mein Projekt fertig ist, (dann) gehe ich sechs Wochen in Urlaub.
wie	Ich weiß nicht mehr, wie ich mit meiner Arbeit zurechtkommen soll.

(→ 📖 C 101.4)

Compare the two sentences.

1. Birsen lernt Deutsch, **denn** sie will bei einer deutschen Firma arbeiten.
2. Birsen will bei einer deutschen Firma arbeiten, **deshalb/deswegen/darum/ daher** lernt sie Deutsch.

The meaning of both sentences is almost identical. However, the clauses in the first sentence are linked with a conjunction. In the second sentence, they are linked with an adverb. An adverb placed at the beginning of a sentence is followed by a verb.

Compare:

	1st position	*2nd position*	
Birsen will in Österreich arbeiten.	Sie	lernt	Deutsch.
Birsen will in Österreich arbeiten.	**Deshalb**	lernt	sie Deutsch.
Birsen will in Österreich arbeiten.	Sie	lernt	**deshalb** Deutsch.

Examples of adverbs that link sentences:

	1st position	*2nd position*	
Ich muss noch arbeiten.	**Außerdem**	habe	ich keine Lust auf Kino.
Ich müsste noch arbeiten.	**Trotzdem**	komme	ich mit ins Kino.
Rolf liest gerne.	**Dagegen**	macht	Rita lieber Sport.
Du musst mehr lernen.	**Sonst**	fällst	du durch.
Henry macht Karate.	**So**	bleibt	er fit und gesund.

More about adverbs in: → 📖 C 90–92.

Bis, seit and während can be used as conjunctions and as prepositions.
Compare the following example sentences:

Conjunction	Es dauerte über eine Stunde, **bis** das Konzert **begann.**
Preposition	Es dauerte über eine Stunde **bis** zum Beginn des Konzerts.

Conjunction	Er arbeitete in der Küche, **während** sie die Zeitung **las.**
Preposition	**Während** des Zeitunglesens durfte man sie nicht stören.

Conjunction	Egon fühlt sich gut, **seit** er zu Hause **arbeitet.**
Preposition	**Seit** fünf Jahren arbeitet Egon zu Hause.

Adverbs

90   Introduction

Read the following text.

Heute war ich in der Stadt. **Zuerst** habe ich mir ein paar Schuhe gekauft. **Dann** bin ich in eine Café gegangen und habe **dort** eine Freundin getroffen. Wir haben uns **lange** unterhalten. **Nachher** sind wir ins Kino gegangen. Der Film war **ziemlich** schlecht. **Trotzdem** sind wir bis zum Schluss geblieben.

Adverbs supply different types of information. Here are some examples:

place (Wo?)	dort, hier, links, rechts, oben, unten, hinten, vorne ...
direction (Wohin?)	hierher, dorthin, (he)rauf, (he)runter ...
time (Wann?)	gestern, heute, jetzt, nachher, zuerst, danach ...
cause (Warum?)	deshalb, darum, daher, deswegen ...
degree	ziemlich, sehr, teilweise ...

Adverbs, unlike adjectives, do not change their form or add endings.
They are not declined and (with few exceptions) have no comparative forms.

91   Comparison of *gern, oft, sehr*

A few adverbs have comparative and superlative forms.
They have almost all been derived from adjectives.

Basic form	gern	oft	sehr
Comparative	lieber	häufiger	mehr
Superlative	am liebsten	am häufigsten	am meisten

The adjectives are:	lieb	häufig	viel

(→ 📖 C 70–71)

The words in bold type in the following dialogues are prepositional adverbs (also known as pronominal adverbs). Their form never changes.

– **Worüber** ärgerst du dich denn so?
+ Dass wir schon wieder Überstunden machen müssen!
– **Darüber** ärgere ich mich auch.

– Sag mal, **wovon** lebt Herr Hug eigentlich?
+ Ich glaube, er kauft und verkauft alte Bücher.
– **Davon** kann man leben?

They consist of

an adverb	and a preposition	
da	an	daran, hieran woran …
hier	auf	darauf, hierauf, worauf …
wo	mit	damit, hiermit, womit …
	von	davon, hiervon, wovon …
	zu	dazu, hierzu, wozu …
	…	

If two vowels meet, an r is inserted between the adverb and the preposition:

da + an = daran   but   da + für = dafür

With prepositional adverbs you can

ask about something: Woran denkst du?

refer to something mentioned previously: Die Ferien waren schön, ich denke oft daran.

refer to something that is about to be mentioned: Denk daran, dass du morgen wieder arbeiten musst.

(→ 📖 C 83)

⚠ Prepositional adverbs can only refer to things or topics, never to people. When referring to people, they are replaced by prepositions and interrogatives:

– **Auf wen** freust du dich denn so?

\+ Auf meine Freundin. Sie kommt morgen nach Hause.

– **Über wen** hast du dich denn geärgert?

\+ Über meinen Chef. Er ist ein richtiges Schwein!

– **Mit wem** arbeitest du zusammen?

\+ Mit Frau Füllemann. Sie ist eine wirklich nette Kollegin.

– **Mit wessen** Auto bist du denn heute gekommen?

\+ Der Mercedes gehört meinem Vater. Er weiß nicht, dass ich damit fahre.

Prepositional adverbs beginning with wo(r) can also be used as relative pronouns.
(→ 📖 C 101.4)

Es gibt nichts, **worauf** er sich noch freuen kann.

Sentences and texts

93 | Introduction

1 Words, sentences, texts

"Incomplete" sentences and reiterations are characteristic of the spoken language. Nevertheless, we rarely fail to understand one another if the situation in which a conversation takes place is clear.
In the written language, the reader is not always immediately aware of the communicative situation, ie why something has been written. For this reason, the written language needs to be clearer and, therefore, "complete" sentences are usually used. In sentences, words are placed in a certain order. Every language has rules which specify the order in which words are placed in sentences.

In this chapter, the most important rules for word order are explained. They will help you to speak and write in a way in which listeners or readers will be able to understand.

| Ich | habe | Hunger |.

| Markieren | Sie | bitte | den Satzakzent |.

However, we do not usually speak in single sentences. Our utterances are usually made up of several sentences. We link sentences together to form a text. There are also rules for forming texts. Some of the more important ones are found at the end of this chapter.

Mutti, ich hab Hunger.
Kannst du mir ein Brot machen?
Eins mit Marmelade, bitte.

Markieren Sie bitte den Satzakzent im Dialog. Lesen Sie ihn dann zu zweit vor.

2 Sentence components

In a sentence, the words are usually grouped into phrases. These word groups are the components of the sentence.

| Meine Freundin und ich | gehen | am Samstag | ins Kino |.

3 Position of the sentence components

Most sentence components can be moved around within a sentence, without changing the basic meaning of the sentence. There are some rules for German word order, particularly for the position of the verb and the nominative complement (subject).

| Ich *(N)* | gehe | am Samstag | ins Kino |.

| Am Samstag | gehe | ich *(N)* | ins Kino |.

| Ins Kino | gehe | ich *(N)* | am Samstag |.

In the following text, there are five different types of sentences.

Ein Mann ging die Straße entlang und lachte.
Warum lachst du?, fragte das Kind.
Muss ich dir darauf antworten?
Sag's mir bitte!
Ich lache, weil ich nicht mehr weinen kann.

2nd position

1. Statement | Ein Mann | *(N)* ⟨ging⟩   die Straße entlang und lachte.

2. Question +   Warum   ⟨lachst⟩ | du | *(N)*?
   interrogative

In statements and questions using an interrogative, the finite verb comes second.

3. Yes-no question   ⟨Muss⟩ | ich | *(N)* dir darauf antworten?

4. Imperative   ⟨Sag⟩   es mir bitte!

In yes-no questions and imperatives, the finite verb comes first.
In yes-no questions, the subject complement comes after the finite verb.

5. Subordinate   ..., weil ich nicht mehr weinen ⟨kann⟩.
   clause

In subordinate clauses, the finite verb comes at the end.

GRAMMAR : 189

95 Verbs and their complements

Every verb requires a least one complement. Usually this is a nominative complement (subject). But there are verbs which require three complements: nominative (N), accusative (A), dative (D) or another complement.

Es *(N)*	regnet.	
Meine Frau *(N)*	ist	Lehrerin *(N).*
Die kleine Katze *(N)*	hat	einen dicken Schwanz *(A).*
Die Kinder *(N)*	schenken	ihren Eltern *(D)* ein neues Fahrrad *(A).*
Ihrem Bruder *(D)*	schenken	sie *(N)* ein Computerspiel *(A).*
Letztes Jahr	waren	wir *(N)* in Frankreich in Urlaub.
Wohin	fahrt	ihr *(N)* dieses Jahr in Urlaub?
	Fliegt	ihr *(N)* nach Kanada?

96 Accusative and dative complements

| Ich | schenke | meinem Bruder *(D)* | ein Buch *(A).* |
| Ich | schenke | ihm *(D)* | ein Buch *(A).* |

The dative complement usually comes before the accusative complement.

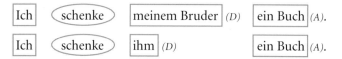

| Ich | schenke | es *(A)* | meinem Bruder *(D).* |
| Ich | schenke | es *(A)* | ihm *(D).* |

If the accusative complement is a pronoun, it comes before the dative complement.

97 The "verbal bracket"

In German, there are verbs or verb groups which consist of several parts. This is the case for compound tenses, separable verbs and verbs in the passive. Generally, the finite verb comes second and the other verb parts come at the end of the sentence.

	2nd position		
Morgen	werde	ich mir einen neuen Computer	kaufen.
Vor zehn Jahren	habe	ich in Kanada	gewohnt.
Der Käse	wird	drei Monate	gelagert.
Wann	bist	du gestern nach Hause	gekommen?
Peter	kommt	morgen nicht	mit ...*
Meine Mutter	will	am Sonntag um drei Uhr wieder	wegfahren.

Sentence 1 Future → 📖 C 19.7
Sentence 2 Perfect → 📖 C 19.5
Sentence 3 Passive → 📖 C 21
Sentence 4 Question + interrogative → 📖 C 52, 103.3
Sentence 5 Separable verb → 📖 C 25.1
Sentence 6 Modal verb → 📖 C 27.2

*Here, there could be a place complement after mit, for example nach Hause / ins Kino / zu mir.

98 Yes-no questions

In yes-no questions, the finite verb comes first. The nominative complement comes immediately after the verb.

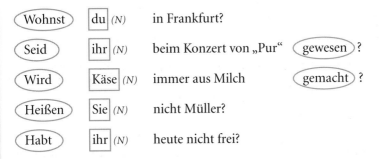

The answer to a positive yes-no question is either Ja or Nein.

– Wohnst du in Frankfurt?   + Ja. / Nein, ich wohne in Chemnitz.

The answer to a negative yes-no question is either Nein or Doch.

– Heißen Sie nicht Müller?   + Doch. / Nein, ich heiße Bühler.

99   Imperatives

In an imperative, the finite verb comes first.

(Schreiben) [Sie] *(N)*   das bitte an die Tafel.

(Gehen)   [wir] *(N)*   doch nach dem Kurs etwas trinken.

In the 1st/3rd person plural, the nominative complement comes directly after the verb.

(Leih) mir *(D)* mal bitte dein Buch.

(Lest) den Dialog *(A)* bitte zu zweit.

For other persons (ie 1st, 2nd, 3rd singular and 2nd plural), no nominative complement is needed.

[Lesen] Sie bitte den Text (mit) .

[Geht] doch mal zusammen (tanzen) .

If a verb has several parts, the finite verb comes first and the other parts come at the end.

100   Main clauses and coordinating conjunctions

[Ich] (schreibe) gern Briefe.   [Ich] (telefoniere) gern.

[Ich] (schreibe) gern Briefe und [ich] (telefoniere) gern.

The main clauses are linked by a conjunction. The word order in both clauses does not change, because the conjunction is a coordinating conjunction.
Here are some more examples:

Statement   [Ich] *(N)* (trinke) Tee, **denn** [Kaffee] *(N)* (schmeckt) mir nicht.

            [Er] *(N)* (isst) gern Kuchen, **aber** [er] *(N)* (darf) keinen essen.

Question   Wo (warst) [du] *(N)* gestern **und** wo (willst) [du] *(N)* jetzt hin?

            (Gehst) [du] *(N)* ins Kino **oder** (triffst) [du] *(N)* dich mit Gabi?

Imperative   (Lesen) [Sie] *(N)* den Text **und** (beantworten) [Sie] *(N)* dann die
            Fragen.

(→ 📖 C 99)

101.1   Introduction

| Hülya |*(N)* (lernt) Deutsch. | Sie |*(N)* (will) in Deutschland studieren.

Both sentences are independent. They are two separate sentences.

| Hülya |*(N)* (lernt) Deutsch, denn | sie |*(N)* (will) in Deutschland studieren.

The compound sentence contains two main clauses linked by a coordinating conjunction.

| Hülya |*(N)* (lernt) Deutsch, weil | sie |*(N)* in Deutschland studieren (will).

The second clause in this sentence cannot stand alone as a sentence.
Clauses that are part of another clause and cannot stand alone are subordinate clauses.

There are four types of subordinate clauses:

subordinate clauses that are introduced by a subordinating conjunction,
subordinate clauses that are introduced by an interrogative,
relative clauses,
infinitive clauses.

101.2   Subordinate clauses introduced by subordinating conjunctions:

| *Main clause* | *Subordinate clause* |

| Der Arzt | (hat) (gesagt), | **dass** | ich |*(N)* weniger (essen) (soll).

| Ich | (kann) nicht weniger (essen), **weil** | mir |*(D)* sonst schlecht (wird).

| Ich | (werde) krank, | **wenn** | ich |*(N)* | Hunger |*(A)* (habe).

The finite verb comes at the end of the clause.

Er ist glücklich,   **weil** | er |*(N)* morgen (wegfährt).

Separable verbs come as an infinitive at the end of the sentence.

(More about conjunctions → 📖 C 84–87, C 89)

101.3 Subordinate clauses introduced by interrogatives

Main clause	Subordinate clause
Ich weiß nicht,	**warum** ich *(N)* so müde (bin).
Ich frage mich,	**wer** *(N)* mein Fahrrad gestohlen (hat).
Fabiane fragt,	**wann** der Kurs *(N)* zu Ende (ist).

Subordinate clauses that are introduced by an interrogative are usually indirect questions. The finite verb comes at the end.

(→ 📖 C 51, 103)

101.4 Relative clauses

A relative clause adds extra information to the noun it refers to in the main clause.

Eine Briefträgerin ist eine Frau , **die** Briefe austrägt.

Relative pronouns introduce relative clauses.

Main clause	Subordinate clause
Das ist das Buch,	**das** ich seit Tagen gesucht habe.
Morgen kommt die Frau zu mir,	**die** früher hier gewohnt hat.
Du musst einen Arzt fragen,	**zu dem** du Vertrauen hast.
Da drüben steht der Mann,	**dessen** Frau wir getroffen haben.

The relative pronoun agrees in gender and number with the noun to which it refers. The verb comes at the end.

Das ist das Lied von „Pur", **von** dem *(D)* ich dir gestern erzählt habe.
Die Freundin, **durch** die *(A)* ich Egon kennen gelernt habe, heißt Moni.

A preposition can precede a relative pronoun.

⚠ If a preposition precedes a relative pronoun, the preposition governs the case of the relative pronoun.
(→ 📖 C 77–83)

The relative clause usually comes immediately after the noun/pronoun to which it refers. For this reason relative clauses can be inserted into main clauses.

Main clause (1st part)	*Relative clause*	*Main clause* (2nd part)
Der Film,	**den** ich gestern gesehen habe,	war langweilig.
Der Mann,	**mit dem** ich in der Disco war,	konnte gut tanzen.

101.5 **Infinitives with** zu **and** um ... zu

Main clause	*Subordinate clause*
Es ist wichtig,	regelmäßig **zu** wiederholen.
Ich halte es für falsch,	jetzt schon auf **zu** geben.
Er fährt nach Kassel,	**um** ins Theater **zu** gehen.

The infinitive with zu usually comes at the end of the sentence.
In infinitive clauses with um ... zu, um introduces the subordinate clause.

Wozu lernt er Deutsch? **Um** einen besseren Job **zu** bekommen.

The subordinate clause with um ... zu indicates purpose in an answer to a question with wozu. (→ 📖 **C 22**)

102 Position of subordinate clauses

There are basically three possibilities for the position of the subordinate clause:

1 The subordinate clause can come after the main clause.

Frau Coban lernt Deutsch, <u>weil sie als Fremdsprachensekretärin arbeitet</u>.

2 The subordinate clause can come before the main clause. In this case, the finite verb in the main clause comes first.

<u>Weil sie als Fremdsprachensekretärin arbeitet</u>, lernt Frau Coban Deutsch.

3 The subordinate clause can be enclosed in the main clause.

Frau Coban, <u>die Deutsch lernt</u>, ist Fremdsprachensekretärin.

103   Reported speech (indirect speech)

103.1   Introduction

Look at this scene on the right.

In reported speech, you can report what someone has said without quoting it in its original form.

103.2   Statements in reported speech

To report something that has been said, a subordinate clause with dass is usually used.(→ 📖 C 101.2)

Direct speech	*Reported speech*
Tom: „Ich habe Hunger.“	Er sagt, **dass** er Hunger hat.
Birsen: „Morgen kaufe ich mir ein neues Fahrrad.“	Birsen hat mir gesagt, **dass** sie sich morgen ein neues Fahrrad kauft.

In spoken German, the indicative is usually used for reported speech.

| Minister of finance: „Die Steuern dürfen nicht erhöht werden.“ | Der Finanzminister stellte fest, dass die Steuern nicht erhöht werden **dürften.** |
| Chairman: „Unsere Firma muss Stellen abbauen.“ | Der Vorsitzende der Tekton GmbH betonte, dass die Firma Stellen abbauen **müsse.** |

In written texts (eg newspapers), however, the subjunctive is often used. (→ 📖 C 20)

Dass can often be omitted. The reported statement is then treated as a main clause. Compare the two sentences:

Der Chef hat gesagt, **dass** du zu ihm kommen sollst .

Der Chef hat gesagt, du sollst zu ihm kommen.

	Main clause	Subordinate clause
1 Yes-no questions	Hast du den Arzt gefragt,	**ob** du rauchen darfst.
	Tina hat mich gefragt,	**ob** du sie morgen besuchst.

When reporting a yes-no question, a subordinate clause with ob is used.

2 Questions with question words

When reporting a question using an interrogative, a subordinate clause with the interrogative is used.

Main clause	Subordinate clause
Hast du den Arzt gefragt,	**wie** viele Tabletten du nehmen musst?
Tina hat mich gefragt,	**wo** du wohnst.

103.4 Imperatives in reported speech

Main clause	Subordinate clause
Der Arzt hat gesagt,	**dass** ich viel Sport machen **soll**.
Tina hat mir gesagt,	**dass** du um drei Uhr bei ihr sein **sollst**.

When reporting an imperative, the modal verb sollen is usually used. The subordinate clause always begins with dass.

104.1 Negation with nicht and kein

Ich habe **nicht** ⎮viel Zeit⎮ *(A)*.

Ich habe **nicht** ⎮die Zeit⎮ *(A)*, dir alles noch einmal zu erklären.

Ich habe ⎮**keine** Zeit⎮ *(A)*.

If the accusative complement is not preceded by a definite article or a determiner, it is negated with a form of kein.

Sandra versteht diese Regel immer noch **nicht**.
Ich habe **kein** Auto. Ich fahre immer mit der Straßenbahn.

Nicht and kein can negate a whole sentence.

Ich arbeite **nicht** bei PEK, sondern bei MTN.
Nicht ich arbeite bei PEK. Mein Bruder arbeitet dort.
Ich esse **kein** Schweinefleisch, aber Huhn esse ich gern.

Nicht and kein can also negate a part of a sentence. They then precede the word they negate.

104.2 Negation with negation words or prefixes

Ich war noch **nie** in China.
Er ist nicht freundlich, sondern **un**freundlich.
Niemand hat meine 500 Urlaubsbilder sehen wollen.
(→ 📖 C 48)

Keiner interessiert sich für meine Urlaubsdias. Und meine Urlaubsgeschichten will auch **keiner** hören.

⚠ In German, double negation means affirmation:

Negation	Er ist **un**freundlich. = Er ist nicht freundlich.
Double negation	Er war **nicht un**freundlich zu mir. = Er war (relativ) freundlich zu mir.

105.1 Introduction

A text is more than simply a series of sentences. Individual sentences are linked to one another. Words in a sentence can refer to something which has already been mentioned, or to something which will be mentioned at a later stage.

Here are some of the most common ways of linking sentences to a text.

Anneliese Bronski ist aus Rostock. Sie besuchte dort neun Jahre die Schule.

Schon während ihrer Schulzeit lernte sie Egon kennen, den sie später hei-

ratete. Nach ihrer Schulzeit machte sie eine Lehre in einer Bäckerei, aber nach

der Lehre bekam sie keinen Job. Deshalb nahm sie eine Stelle als Verkäuferin in

einem Supermarkt an. 1996 bekam sie ihr erstes Kind. Seitdem ist sie zu Hause.

Wenn das Kind in den Kindergarten kommt, will sie noch einmal zur Schule

gehen und vielleicht eine Ausbildung als Internet-Kundenberaterin machen.

Diese Ausbildung dauert ein Jahr. Sie wird vom Arbeitsamt bezahlt.

The highlighted words link individual clauses and sentences to a text. In this text, personal pronouns (sie), possessive pronouns (ihr), relative pronouns (den), demonstrative pronouns (diese), conjunctions (und, aber, wenn) and adverbs (dort, deshalb, seitdem) have been used.

Links with pronouns

Pronouns often link several sentences to one another. ($\rightarrow$ 📖 C 100–101)

Die Telekom ist eine große deutsche Telefongesellschaft. **Sie** gehört zu den

vier größten Telekommunikationskonzernen der Welt. **Ihre** Aktien werden

an der Börse gehandelt. Der Kurs **dieser** Aktien ist stark gestiegen.

Definite and indefinite articles

The definite article is used if the listener or reader already knows the subject of the sentence. The indefinite article is used when introducing a subject for the first time. ($\rightarrow$ 📖 C 40–42)

Anneliese Bronski suchte dringend **eine Stelle**. **Der Job** im Supermarkt gefiel

ihr zwar nicht, aber so konnte sie wenigstens etwas eigenes Geld verdienen.

Conjunctions

Conjunctions can link words, clauses and sentences. Usually, they also determine the way in which the individual sections are related to one another, ie complements, contradictions, sequences, etc ($\rightarrow$ 📖 C 84–89, C 100–101)

Sie machte eine Lehre als Bäckerin, **aber** sie bekam danach keine Stelle,

weil immer mehr Brot in Fabriken gebacken wird.

Adverbs

Adverbs, like conjunctions, can represent relationships between words or sentences, ie time, succession, reason, etc ($\rightarrow$ 📖 C 90–92)

1996 bekam Anneliese ein Kind. **Seitdem** ist sie zu Hause. **Später** will sie aber

wieder arbeiten. **Deshalb** bereitet sie sich jetzt schon auf eine Ausbildung als

Internet-Kundenberaterin vor.

APPENDIX

1 Numbers

1.1 Cardinal numbers and ordinal numbers (→ 📖 C 73–76)

0	null		
1	eins	(der/das/die) 1.	erste (Mann/Kind/Frau)
2	zwei	2.	zweite
3	drei	3.	dritte
4	vier	4.	vierte
5	fünf	5.	fünfte
6	sechs	6.	sechste
7	sieben	7.	siebte
8	acht	8.	achte
9	neun	9.	neunte
10	zehn	10.	zehnte
11	elf	11.	elfte
12	zwölf	12.	zwölfte
13	dreizehn	13.	dreizehnte
14	vierzehn	14.	vierzehnte
15	fünfzehn	15.	fünfzehnte
16	sechzehn	16.	sechzehnte
17	siebzehn	17.	siebzehnte
18	achtzehn	18.	achtzehnte
19	neunzehn	19.	neunzehnte
20	zwanzig	20.	zwanzigste
21	einundzwanzig	21.	einundzwanzigste
22	zweiundzwanzig	22.	zweiundzwanzigste
23	dreiundzwanzig	23.	dreiundzwanzigste
30	dreißig	30.	dreißigste
31	einunddreißig	31.	einunddreißigste
40	vierzig	40.	vierzigste
50	fünfzig	50.	fünfzigste
60	sechzig	60.	sechzigste
70	siebzig	70.	siebzigste
80	achzig	80.	achzigste
90	neunzig	90.	neunzigste
100	einhundert	100.	einhundertste
101	einhundertundeins	101.	einhundertunderste
200	zweihundert	200.	zweihundertste
1 000	eintausend	1 000.	eintausendste
1 001	eintausendundeins	1 001.	eintausendunderste
1 100	eintausendeinhundert	1 100.	eintausendeinhundertste
10 001	zehntausendundeins	10 001.	zehntausendunderste
100 000	einhunderttausend	100 000.	einhunderttausendste
1 000 000	eine Million	1 000 000.	millionste

1.2 Percentages, decimals and fractions

12 %	Die Arbeitslosenquote lag 1997 bei ungefähr **zwölf Prozent**.
74,7 %	**Vierundsiebzig Komma sieben Prozent** der Österreicherinnen und Österreicher haben eine Tageszeitung.
1,25 %	Die Inflationsrate wird in diesem Jahr bei **eins Komma zwei fünf Prozent** liegen.
0,5 ‰	Wer Auto fährt, darf in den meisten Staaten der EU nicht mehr als 0,5 **Promille** Alkohol im Blut haben.
4,8 Mio.	**Vier Komma acht Millionen** Menschen waren 1997 in Deutschland arbeitslos.
10,49 sec	Der Weltrekord über 100 Meter Sprint der Frauen lag 1997 bei **zehn Komma vier neun Sekunden.**
8,90 m	Der Weltrekord im Weitsprung lag 1997 bei **acht Meter neunzig.**
$^1/_2$	ein halb
$^1/_3$	ein Drittel
$^1/_4$, $^1/_5$	ein Viertel, ein Fünftel …
$^1/_{100}$	ein Hundertstel
$^1/_{1000}$	ein Tausendstel
$1^1/_2$	eineinhalb

1.3 Weights, measures and money

1 mm	ein Millimeter	1,50 Euro	ein Euro fünfzig (Deutschland, Österreich)
1 cm	ein Zentimeter		
1 m	ein Meter	0,40 Euro	vierzig Cent (Deutschland, Österreich)
1,30 m	ein Meter dreißig		
1 km	ein Kilometer		
		5,00 DM	fünf (Deutsche) Mark (Deutschland)
100 km/h	einhundert Stundenkilometer / Kilometer pro Stunde	0,30 DM	dreißig Pfennig (Deutschland)
1 m²	ein Quadratmeter		
1 m³	ein Kubikmeter	2,00 ÖS	zwei Schilling (Österreich)
		0,20 ÖS	zwanzig Groschen (Österreich)
1 g	ein Gramm		
1 Pfd.	ein Pfund (500 g)		
1 kg	ein Kilo = Kilogramm (1000 g)	5,60 SFr	fünf Franken sechzig (Schweiz)
1 l	ein Liter	0,50 SFr	fünfzig Rappen (Schweiz)
1 °C	ein Grad Celsius		
− 5 °C	minus fünf Grad Celsius / fünf Grad unter null		
+ 30 °C	plus dreißig Grad Celsius / dreißig Grad warm		

2 Verbs with prepositions

2.1 Verbs with prepositions taking the accusative

Verb	Preposition	Example
abstimmen	über	Wir müssen über diesen Antrag abstimmen.
achten	auf	Achten Sie auf den Satzanfang.
ankommen	auf	Es kommt auf jeden Einzelnen an.
antworten	auf	Antworte bitte auf meine Frage.
sich ärgern	über	Ich habe mich sehr über diesen Mann geärgert.
aufpassen	auf	Du musst besser auf deinen Hund aufpassen.
sich aufregen	über	Ständig regen sich die Leute über meinen Hund auf.
ausgeben	für	Ich gebe viel Geld für Bücher aus.
sich bedanken	für	Sie bedankte sich für das Geschenk.
sich bemühen	um	Ich habe mich lange um eine Wohnung bemüht.
beraten	über	Wir müssen über diesen Plan beraten.
berichten	über	Der Polizist berichtet über den Unfall.
beschließen	über	Über diese Punkte muss das Gericht beschließen.
sich beschweren	über	Er beschwerte sich über den Lärm.
sich bewerben	um	Ich habe mich einen neuen Job beworben.
sich beziehen	auf	Ich beziehe mich auf Ihren Brief.
bitten	um	Darf ich Sie um einen Rat bitten?
danken	für	Ich danke dir für deinen Hinweis.
denken	an	Sie denkt oft an ihren Freund.
diskutieren	über	Wir diskutieren morgen über diesen Vorschlag.
sich drehen	um	Alles dreht sich um diesen Mann.
sich eignen	für	Ich eigne mich nicht für diesen Beruf.
sich entscheiden	für	Sie entschied sich für die billigere Wohnung.
sich entschuldigen	für	Ich entschuldige mich für diesen Fehler.
erinnern	an	Sie erinnert mich an meine Mutter.
sich erinnern	an	Sie erinnerte sich plötzlich an ihren Termin.
ersetzen	durch	Wir müssen Herrn Dupont durch einen anderen Mitarbeiter ersetzen.
folgen	auf	Welcher Monat folgt auf den Mai?
sich freuen	auf	Ich freue mich immer besonders auf den Samstag.
sich freuen	über	Sie freut sich über jeden Brief, den sie bekommt.
gehen	um	In diesem Buch geht es um einen bekannten Mann.
sich gewöhnen	an	Ich habe mich an den Lärm hier gewöhnt.
glauben	an	Kinder glauben an den Osterhasen.
halten	für	Halten Sie ihn für einen Verbrecher?
sich halten	an	Ich halte mich an deinen Rat.
sich halten	für	Du hältst dich wohl für etwas Besseres?
sich handeln	um	Ich möchte Sie sprechen. Es handelt sich um den neuen Job.
hoffen	auf	Wir hoffen auf einen schönen Sommer.
informieren	über	Wir möchten Sie über unseren Plan informieren.

Verb	Preposition	Example
sich informieren	über	Ich möchte mich lieber selber über den Job informieren.
sich interessieren	für	Sie interessiert sich für meine Briefmarken.
kämpfen	für	Die Arbeiter kämpfen für einen höheren Lohn.
kämpfen	gegen	Sie kämpft gegen den Schlaf, aber ohne Erfolg.
kämpfen	um	Die Zuschauer kämpfen um einen guten Platz.
klagen	über	Er klagt über Kopfschmerzen.
kommen	auf	Wie bist du auf diesen Vorschlag gekommen?
sich kümmern	um	Wer kümmert sich um dich, wenn ich weg bin?
lächeln	über	Sie lächelt über den Witz.
lachen	über	Die Leute lachen über den Clown.
nachdenken	über	Ich habe lange über den Vorschlag nachgedacht.
protestieren	gegen	Ich protestiere gegen diesen Entscheid!
reagieren	auf	Sie reagierte mit Lachen auf seinen Vorschlag.
reden	über	Ich will nicht immer nur über den Chef reden.
schimpfen	über	Sie schimpfte über den Lärm.
sein	für	Ich war für weniger Arbeit und einen höheren Lohn.
sein	gegen	Er war gegen den neuen Computer.
sorgen	für	Er sorgt gut für seinen Vater.
sich sorgen	um	Sie sorgt sich um ihren kranken Hund.
sprechen	über	Die Lehrerin möchte über den Kurs sprechen.
stellen	auf	Stell den Schalter auf die Stufe 3.
stimmen	für	Viele stimmten für den neuen Plan.
stimmen	gegen	Einige stimmten gegen den Plan.
streiten	über	Über Geschmack kann man nicht streiten.
tun	für	Würdest du das für mich tun?
sich unterhalten	über	Wir haben uns lange über ihn unterhalten.
unterrichten	über	Man hat mich über den Plan unterrichtet.
sich verlassen	auf	Auf mich können Sie sich verlassen!
sich verlieben	in	Peter hat sich in mich verliebt.
vermieten	an	Sie haben das Haus an ihren Sohn vermietet.
verzichten	auf	Sie hat auf ihren freien Tag verzichtet.
sich vorbereiten	auf	Du solltest dich gut auf den Test vorbereiten.
wählen	in	Er wurde nicht in den Rat gewählt.
warten	auf	Ich kann nicht mehr länger auf ihn warten.
sich wenden	an	Wenden Sie sich doch an den Polizisten dort.
sich wundern	über	Er hat sich sehr über den Vorschlag gewundert.

2.2 Verbs with prepositions taking the dative

Verb	Preposition	Example
abhängen	von	Es hängt vom Wetter ab, ob wir einen Ausflug machen.
abheben	von	Ich möchte 300 DM von meinem Konto abheben.
ändern	an	An dieser Situation kann man nichts ändern.
anfangen	mit	Wann fängst du mit der Arbeit an?
auffordern	zu	Sie hat ihn zum Tanzen aufgefordert.
aufhören	mit	Hör endlich mit dem Gejammer auf!
sich auseinander setzen	mit	Wir müssen uns mit ihm auseinander setzen.
beginnen	mit	Wann beginnst du mit deiner Arbeit?
sich beschäftigen	mit	Sie beschäftigt sich am liebsten mit ihrem Hund.
bestehen	aus	Band 1 besteht aus 24 Einheiten.
einladen	zu	Er lädt mich zum Abendessen ein.
sich entschließen	zu	Sie hat sich zu diesem Schritt entschlossen.
sich entwickeln	zu	Er hat sich zu einem guten Mitarbeiter entwickelt.
sich erholen	von	Sie hat sich gut von dem Unfall erholt.
sich erkundigen	nach	Er erkundigte sich nach seinem Kontostand.
erzählen	von	Bitte erzähl mir mehr von dir!
erziehen	zu	Seine Eltern haben ihn zu einem netten Menschen erzogen.
fehlen	an	Unserer Firma fehlt es an Aufträgen.
folgen	aus	Aus diesem Bericht folgt, dass es der Firma wieder besser geht.
fragen	nach	Er hat schon oft nach meinem Mann gefragt.
führen	zu	Diese Diskussion führt zu keinem Resultat.
sich fürchten	vor	Ich fürchte mich nicht vor Mäusen.
gehören	zu	Gehörst du auch zu dieser Klasse?
gratulieren	zu	Ich gratuliere dir zum Geburtstag.
halten	von	Was halten Sie von diesem Vorschlag?
handeln	mit	Die Firma handelt mit wilden Tieren.
handeln	von	Der Film handelt von Mäusen und Menschen.
hindern	an	Das Telefon hindert mich an der Arbeit.
hören	von	Ich habe schon viel von Ihnen gehört.
sich irren	in	Entschuldigung, ich habe mich wohl in der Telefonnummer geirrt.
kommen	zu	Wegen des Nebels kam es zu vielen Unfällen.
leben	von	Er lebt von seiner Rente.
leiden	an	Er leidet an einer Krankheit.
leiden	unter	Er leidet unter der Hitze.
liegen	an	Es liegt am Wetter, dass ich Kopfschmerzen habe.
meinen	zu	Was meinen Sie zu meinem Vorschlag?
sich melden	bei	Melden Sie sich bitte beim Sekretariat?
passen	zu	Dieser Hut passt nicht zu deinem Kleid!
profitieren	von	Er hat viel von ihr profitiert.

Verb	Preposition	Example
rechnen	mit	Ich habe schon nicht mehr mit dir gerechnet.
reden	von	Alle reden nur noch von diesem Film.
sich richten	nach	Ich kann mich nicht immer nach dir richten.
riechen	nach	Mmh, hier riecht es nach deinem Parfum.
rufen	nach	Er rief laut nach seinem Hund.
schimpfen	mit	Bitte schimpf nicht mit mir!
schließen	aus	Ich schließe aus ihrem Blick, dass sie glücklich ist.
schmecken	nach	Dieses Eis schmeckt nach Äpfeln.
schützen	vor	Vitamin C soll vor vielen Krankheiten schützen.
sich schützen	vor	Sie sollten sich vor dem kalten Wind schützen.
sehen	nach	Ich sehe mal schnell nach dem Kuchen im Ofen.
sich sehnen	nach	Ich sehne mich nach dir.
sprechen	mit	Mit wem sprichst du?
sprechen	von	Es spricht gern von seinen Kindern.
sich streiten	mit	Er streitet sich oft mit ihr.
teilnehmen	an	Nimmst du auch am nächsten Kurs teil?
telefonieren	mit	Mit wem telefonierst du?
träumen	von	Gestern habe ich von dir geträumt.
sich treffen	mit	Ich werde mich heute mit einem Freund treffen.
trennen	von	Man trennt die jungen Kätzchen von ihrer Mutter.
sich trennen	von	Du sollest dich von ihm trennen.
überreden	zu	Der Verkäufer hat mich zum Kauf überredet.
sich unterhalten	mit	Er hat sich lange mit seiner Chefin unterhalten.
unterscheiden	von	Ich kann Maria nicht von Eva unterscheiden.
sich unterscheiden	von	Er unterscheidet sich stark von seinem Vater.
sich verabreden	mit	Ich habe mich mit ihm verabredet.
sich verabschieden	von	So, jetzt muss ich mich von dir verabschieden.
verbinden	mit	Verbinden Sie die Punkte mit einer Linie.
vergleichen	mit	Vergleichen Sie die Kopie mit dem Original.
sich verloben	mit	Sie hat sich gestern mit ihrem Freund verlobt.
verstehen	von	Sie versteht viel von der deutschen Literatur.
sich verstehen	mit	Sie versteht sich gut mit ihm.
verwechseln	mit	Ich habe Sie leider mit jemandem verwechselt.
wählen	zu	Eine Frau wurde gestern zur Präsidentin gewählt.
wählen	zwi-schen	Sie können zwischen dem Menü 1 und 2 wählen.
warnen	vor	Ich warne dich vor diesem Mann.
werden	zu	Er wurde zu einem Experten.
wissen	von	Wissen Sie schon von unserem Plan?
zweifeln	an	Zweifelst du etwa an meinen Fähigkeiten?
zwingen	zu	Man zwingt den Politiker zum Rücktritt.

Infinitive	*Present*	*Simple past*	*Perfect*
abreiben	er reibt ab	er rieb ab	er hat abgerieben
anfangen	er fängt an	er fing an	er hat angefangen
anstreichen	er streicht an	er strich an	er hat angestrichen
backen	er backt/bäckt	er backte	er hat gebacken
befehlen	er befiehlt	er befahl	er hat befohlen
beginnen	er beginnt	er begann	er hat begonnen
begreifen	er begreift	er begriff	er hat begriffen
beißen	er beißt	es biss	er hat gebissen
beweisen	er beweist	er bewies	er hat bewiesen
biegen	er biegt	er bog	er hat den Ast gebogen
			er ist um die Ecke gebogen
bieten	er bietet	er bot	er hat geboten
bitten	er bittet	er bat	er hat gebeten
bleiben	er bleibt	er blieb	er ist geblieben
braten	er brät	er briet	er hat gebraten
brechen	er bricht	er brach	er hat das Bein gebrochen
			das Eis ist gebrochen
brennen	er brennt	er brannte	er hat gebrannt
bringen	er bringt	er brachte	er hat gebracht
denken	er denkt	er dachte	er hat gedacht
durchstreichen	er streicht durch	er strich durch	er hat durchgestrichen
dürfen	ich darf	ich durfte	er hat gedurft
	du darfst	du durftest	er hat arbeiten dürfen
	er/es/sie darf	er/es/sie durfte	
	wir dürfen	wir durften	
	ihr dürft	ihr durftet	
	sie dürfen	sie durften	
einladen	er lädt ein	er lud ein	er hat eingeladen
empfangen	er empfängt	er empfing	er hat empfangen
empfehlen	er empfiehlt	er empfahl	er hat empfohlen
empfinden	er empfindet	er empfand	er hat empfunden
entscheiden	er entscheidet	er entschied	er hat entschieden
erschrecken	er erschrickt	er erschrak	er ist erschrocken
essen	er isst	er aß	er hat gegessen
fahren	er fährt	er fuhr	er ist nach China gefahren
			er hat das Auto gefahren
fallen	er fällt	er fiel	er ist gefallen
finden	er findet	er fand	er hat gefunden
fliegen	er fliegt	er flog	er ist nach Rom geflogen
			er hat das Flugzeug geflogen
fließen	er fließt	er floss	er ist geflossen
fressen	er frisst	er fraß	er hat gefressen
frieren	er friert	er fror	er hat gefroren
geben	er gibt	er gab	er hat gegeben

Infinitive	Present	Simple past	Perfect
gehen	er geht	er ging	er ist gegangen
gelingen	er gelingt	er gelang	er ist gelungen
gelten	er gilt	er galt	er hat gegolten
genießen	er genießt	er genoss	er hat genossen
geschehen	er geschieht	er geschah	er ist geschehen
gewinnen	er gewinnt	er gewann	er hat gewonnen
haben	ich habe	ich hatte	er hat gehabt
	du hast	du hattest	
	er/es/sie hat	er/es/sie hatte	
	wir haben	wir hatten	
	ihr habt	ihr hattet	
	sie haben	sie hatten	
halten	er hält	er hielt	er hat gehalten
hängen	er hängt	er hing	er hat gehangen
heben	er hebt	er hob	er hat gehoben
heißen	er heißt	er hieß	er hat geheißen
helfen	er hilft	er half	er hat geholfen
kennen	er kennt	er kannte	er hat gekannt
klingen	er klingt	er klang	er hat geklungen
kommen	er kommt	er kam	er ist gekommen
können	ich kann	ich konnte	er hat gekonnt
	du kannst	du konntest	er hat arbeiten können
	er/es/sie kann	er/es/sie konnte	
	wir können	wir konnten	
	ihr könnt	ihr konntet	
	sie können	sie konnten	
lassen	er lässt	er ließ	er hat gelassen
			er hat ihn arbeiten lassen
laufen	er läuft	er lief	er ist gelaufen
leiden	er leidet	er litt	er hat gelitten
leihen	er leiht	er lieh	er hat geliehen
lesen	er liest	er las	er hat gelesen
liegen	er liegt	er lag	er hat im Bett gelegen
			das Dorf ist schön gelegen
lügen	er lügt	er log	er hat gelogen
mahlen	er mahlt	er mahlte	er hat gemahlen
messen	er misst	er maß	er hat gemessen
mögen	ich mag	ich mochte	er hat gemocht
	du magst	du mochtest	er hat arbeiten mögen
	er/es/sie mag	er/es/sie mochte	
	wir mögen	wir mochten	
	ihr mögt	ihr mochtet	
	sie mögen	sie mochten	

Infinitive	Present	Simple past	Perfect
müssen	ich muss	ich musste	er hat gemusst
	du musst	du musstest	er hat arbeiten müssen
	er/es/sie muss	er/es/sie musste	
	wir müssen	wir mussten	
	ihr müsst	ihr musstet	
	sie müssen	sie mussten	
nehmen	er nimmt	er nahm	er hat genommen
nennen	er nennt	er nannte	er hat genannt
pfeifen	er pfeift	er pfiff	er hat gepfiffen
raten	er rät	er riet	er hat geraten
riechen	er riecht	er roch	er hat gerochen
rufen	er ruft	er rief	er hat gerufen
schaffen	er schafft	er schuf	er hat geschaffen
scheinen	er scheint	er schien	er hat geschienen
schieben	er schiebt	er schob	er hat geschoben
schießen	er schießt	er schoss	er hat geschossen
schlafen	er schläft	er schlief	er hat geschlafen
schlagen	er schlägt	er schlug	er hat geschlagen
schleifen	er schleift	er schliff	er hat geschliffen
schließen	er schließt	er schloss	er hat geschlossen
schneiden	er schneidet	er schnitt	er hat geschnitten
schreiben	er schreibt	er schrieb	er hat geschrieben
schreien	er schreit	er schrie	er hat geschrien
schwimmen	er schwimmt	er schwamm	er ist geschwommen
sehen	er sieht	er sah	er hat gesehen
			er hat ihn kommen sehen
sein	ich bin	ich war	er ist gewesen
	du bist	du warst	
	er/es/sie ist	er/es/sie war	
	wir sind	wir waren	
	ihr seid	ihr wart	
	sie sind	sie waren	
singen	er singt	er sang	er hat gesungen
sinken	er sinkt	er sank	er ist gesunken
sitzen	er sitzt	er saß	er hat gesessen
sollen	ich soll	ich sollte	er hat gesollt
	du sollst	du solltest	er hat arbeiten sollen
	er/es/sie soll	er/es/sie sollte	
	wir sollen	wir sollten	
	ihr sollt	ihr solltet	
	sie sollen	sie sollten	
spinnen	er spinnt	er spann	er hat gesponnen
sprechen	er spricht	er sprach	er hat gesprochen
springen	er springt	er sprang	er ist gesprungen
stechen	er sticht	er stach	er hat gestochen
stehen	er steht	er stand	er hat gestanden

Infinitive	Present	Simple past	Perfect
stehlen	er stiehlt	er stahl	er hat gestohlen
steigen	er steigt	er stieg	er ist gestiegen
sterben	er stirbt	er starb	er ist gestorben
stinken	er stinkt	er stank	er hat gestunken
streiten	er streitet	er stritt	er hat gestritten
tragen	er trägt	er trug	er hat getragen
treffen	er trifft	er traf	er hat getroffen
treiben	er treibt	er trieb	er hat getrieben
treten	er tritt	er trat	er hat getreten
trinken	er trinkt	er trank	er hat getrunken
tun	er tut	er tat	er hat getan
überweisen	er überweist	er überwies	er hat überwiesen
unterstreichen	er unterstreicht	er unterstrich	er hat unterstrichen
verbinden	er verbindet	er verband	er hat verbunden
vergessen	er vergisst	er vergaß	er hat vergessen
vergleichen	er vergleicht	er verglich	er hat verglichen
verlieren	er verliert	er verlor	er hat verloren
vermeiden	er vermeidet	er vermied	er hat vermieden
verschwinden	er verschwindet	er verschwand	er ist verschwunden
verzeihen	er verzeiht	er verzieh	er hat verziehen
wachsen	er wächst	er wuchs	er ist gewachsen
waschen	er wäscht	er wusch	er hat gewaschen
werden	ich werde	ich wurde	er ist geworden
	du wirst	du wurdest	er ist gefragt worden
	er/es/sie wird	er/es/sie wurde	
	wir werden	wir wurden	
	ihr werdet	ihr wurdet	
	sie werden	sie wurden	
werfen	er wirft	er warf	er hat geworfen
wiegen	er wiegt	er wog	er hat gewogen
wissen	ich weiß	ich wusste	er hat gewusst
	du weißt	du wusstest	
	er/es/sie weiß	er/es/sie wusste	
	wir wissen	wir wussten	
	ihr wisst	ihr wusstet	
	sie wissen	sie wussten	
wollen	ich will	ich wollte	er hat gewollt
	du willst	du wolltest	er hat arbeiten wollen
	er/es/sie will	er/es/sie wollte	
	wir wollen	wir wollten	
	ihr wollt	ihr wolltet	
	sie wollen	sie wollten	
ziehen	er zieht	er zog	er hat den Wagen gezogen
			er ist aufs Land gezogen
zwingen	er zwingt	er zwang	er hat gezwungen

Index

The numbers represent page numbers.

Illustration credits

AP: © Shapiro, S. 40 – © Becht, U1 – © Bertelsmann Lexikon-Verlag, Gütersloh, „Das große Bilderlexikon der Vögel" von J. Hanzak, S. 174 (rechts) – © Bongarts, S. 154 – © Cornelsen, Lücking, S. 12, S. 120 – © Diogenes Verlag, Zürich, „Der fliegende Robert", aus: „Der Struwwelpeter oder Lustige Geschichten und drollige Bilder von Dr. Heinrich Hoffmann", S. 102 – Image Bank: © Castañeda, S. 135 (rechts); © Lockyer, S. 96; © de Lossy, S. 199 – © Karthographisches Institut Bertelsmann, aus: „neuer atlas der welt", S. 91 (oben) – Okapia: © Danegger, S. 174 (links); © Mercieca, S. 174 (Mitte) – © Rohrmann, S. 27, S. 67, S. 83, S. 84, S. 85, S. 89, S. 178, S. 185 – Ullstein: © Bonn-Sequenz, S. 116; © CARO/Jandke, S. 123; © dpa, S. 135 (links) © Melde Press, S. 119 (links); © Peters, S. 119 (rechts) – © Verlag Benedikt Taschen, Köln, „Die vier Jahreszeiten" von Guiseppe Arcimboldo, S. 99.

Permissions

© Cornelsen & Oxford University Press, Berlin, aus: „Das Oxford Schulwörterbuch, English-German, Deutsch-Englisch", S. 117 – © Insel Verlag, Frankfurt a. M., Mark Twain zitiert nach Herbert Genzmer: „Deutsche Grammatik", S. 171 – © Langenscheidt, München, aus: „Langenscheidts Eurowörterbuch Portugiesisch", S. 47 (oben und unten), S. 144; aus: „Langenscheidt Großwörterbuch Deutsch als Fremdsprache", S. 48, S. 136, S. 142 (Mitte links und rechts), S. 156 (unten); aus Heinz Messinger: „Langenscheidts Großwörterbuch Der Kleine Muret-Sanders, Deutsch-Englisch", S. 156 (oben) – © Suhrkamp Verlag, Frankfurt a. M., Ernst Bloch, aus: „Spuren", S. 150.

Nicht alle Copyrightinhaber konnten ermittelt werden; deren Urheberrechte werden hiermit vorsorglich und ausdrücklich anerkannt.